W9-AXQ-536

WEATHER 101

FROM DOPPLER RADAR AND **LONG-RANGE FORECASTS** TO THE **POLAR VORTEX** AND **CLIMATE CHANGE,** EVERYTHING YOU NEED TO KNOW ABOUT THE **STUDY OF WEATHER**

KATHLEEN SEARS

Demo

Adams Media

New York London Toronto Sydney New Delhi

Adams Media
An Imprint of Simon & Schuster, Inc.
57 Littlefield Street
Avon, Massachusetts 02322

Copyright © 2017 by Simon & Schuster, Inc.

All rights reserved, including the right to reproduce this book or portions thereof in any form whatsoever. For information address Adams Media Subsidiary Rights Department, 1230 Avenue of the Americas, New York, NY 10020.

First Adams Media hardcover edition SEPTEMBER 2017

ADAMS MEDIA and colophon are trademarks of Simon and Schuster.

For information about special discounts for bulk purchases, please contact Simon & Schuster Special Sales at 1-866-506-1949 or business@simonandschuster.com.

The Simon & Schuster Speakers Bureau can bring authors to your live event. For more information or to book an event contact the Simon & Schuster Speakers Bureau at 1-866-248-3049 or visit our website at www.simonspeakers.com.

Manufactured in the United States of America

10 9 8 7 6 5 4 3 2

Library of Congress Cataloging-in-Publication Data has been applied for.

ISBN 978-1-5072-0463-4
ISBN 978-1-5072-0464-1 (ebook)

Many of the designations used by manufacturers and sellers to distinguish their products are claimed as trademarks. Where those designations appear in this book and Simon & Schuster, Inc., was aware of a trademark claim, the designations have been printed with initial capital letters.

Contains material adapted from the following title published by Adams Media, an Imprint of Simon & Schuster, Inc.: *The Everything® Weather Book* by Mark Cantrell, copyright © 2002, ISBN 978-1-58062-668-2.

CONTENTS

Demo

INTRODUCTION

Lightning. Supercells. Blizzards. All of it's weather, and all of it affects your life. But what exactly *is* weather?

It's one of the most complicated and difficult-to-predict systems in existence. Since the beginning of the human race, people have tried to understand it in order to benefit from good weather and protect themselves from bad. Today's scientists have come a long way in predicting major weather events, but they still can't make accurate long-term forecasts.

This is despite the fact that there's a lot of information today about the weather: it's on television, on the radio, in newspapers, blogs, vlogs, and on *YouTube*. That's why many people want to know more about how weather works.

In *Weather 101* you'll find out such things as:

- The causes of storms such as hurricanes and tornadoes
- What the different kinds of clouds mean
- What terms like "high-pressure front," "the jet stream," and "El Niño" mean
- How to stay safe in a storm

Weather 101 will also tackle issues like pollution, acid rain, damage to the ozone layer, and climate change. The more you learn about the weather, the stranger things you'll find: from supercells to exotic lightning forms (called sprites, elves, and blue jets), from polar vortices to microbursts. Scientists have developed sophisticated devices to study and measure all these things and more; including not only instruments here on Earth but also weather satellites that can look at atmospheric changes from space. All of this helps them understand the complexity and ever-changing nature of weather systems—and relay this information to you so you can plan accordingly: everything from your vacation to when to start your drive to work in the morning.

If you're fascinated by the range of global weather patterns, if you want to learn about important weather-related disasters, or if you just want to know how to cope with the weather in your area, you'll find the answers to your questions in *Weather 101*.

Knowing more about the weather isn't just important—it's *essential* in our rapidly changing world. It's time to get started.

WHY DO WE HAVE WEATHER?

Something We All Have in Common

"Don't knock the weather; nine-tenths of the people couldn't start a conversation if it didn't change once in a while."

—Kin Hubbard, US journalist, humorist

Simply put, weather is what's going on in the atmosphere in any one location at a particular time. Understanding weather allows us to plan our day, our vacations, and our crops. And it's a handy conversation starter.

WHY IT'S A BIG DEAL

In fact, weather is a complex and dynamic process driven by the Sun; the earth's oceans, rotation, and inclination; and so many other factors that many of its mysteries still remain unexplained. Being prepared for what the weather brings can be as simple as turning on the TV to catch the latest forecast before heading for the beach, or as complicated as examining long-range forecasts to decide which crops to plant. Weather constantly affects people in small ways, but weather can also have major consequences when hurricanes or tornadoes threaten their well-being and livelihoods, or even their lives.

The weather can even affect your health, especially during extremes in temperature or precipitation. If you're not dressed properly in cold weather, you can fall victim to hypothermia, which occurs when the body's core temperature drops below the point where things function normally. The flip side of hypothermia is hyperthermia, where the body's core temperature rises too high. Hyperthermia can cause heat exhaustion or even heat stroke, which can be fatal.

A Cold? Or Allergies?

During the summer, a stuffy nose and postnasal drip may have you convinced you're suffering from a cold. But the same symptoms may be due to allergies. Remember that colds last an average of three to seven days, while allergic reactions can go on for ten days to several weeks. If you're still miserable after a week, chances are you've got allergies.

Weather can also affect your health in less obvious ways. Long spells of gray winter weather can lead to seasonal affective disorder (SAD), a malady that causes depression and a debilitating lack of energy; it's thought to be caused by lower light levels during the winter as the days become shorter and the Sun rises lower in the sky. Many arthritis sufferers complain of worsening symptoms when atmospheric pressure falls, and there is a statistical rise in the number of heart attacks after abrupt weather changes such as passing storm fronts.

THE BIG PICTURE

On a larger scale, weather plays a big role in the economic health of every nation on Earth. A timely soaking rain can rescue a crop from ruin, while a sudden torrential cloudburst can wash it away. And farmers aren't the only ones at risk; those who depend on natural gas for heat often watch in dismay as a particularly cold winter sends prices skyward. Hurricanes can drive tourists away from areas that depend on a regular influx of visitors for their livelihoods. Even a gentle phenomenon like fog can result in disaster, as the captains of the *Andrea Doria* and the *Stockholm* learned one fateful July night in 1956. And during the Dust Bowl of 1936, one of the hottest and driest summers ever recorded, more than 15,000 people died of malnutrition and dust-related diseases.

Ancient Hurricanes

Scientists look for evidence of ancient hurricanes in a branch of science called paleotempestology. Evidence of past storms can be found in coral skeletons, sediments from the ocean bottom, and even in caves, where stalactites retain the chemical signatures of abrupt cloudbursts caused by tropical cyclones.

With a growing realization of the weather's importance and so much weather news readily available on TV and the Internet, it's no wonder that interest in the subject is soaring. It seems that almost every day a weather disaster is happening somewhere in the world. Yet it's important to remember that extreme weather events, from droughts to hurricanes, have been happening for millennia, long before there were cameras to record them or buildings and people to get in their way.

One of the reasons weather is so compelling is because it is universal: snow falls just as heavily on poor neighborhoods as it does in well-to-do suburbs, and a flash flood can destroy both mansions and shacks with equal force. Weather is the one thing everyone has in common.

WEATHER AND CIVILIZATION

A Historical Force

Ancient people did their best to understand and predict the weather. Lacking modern scientific instruments, early civilizations observed nature and kept records of the seasons. They understood how important the Sun was for growing their crops, which explains why many ancient cultures worshiped sun gods. In Mesopotamia the Babylonians counted on the weather gods Hadad and Marduk to bring them good harvests. The Hittites left the weather-producing chores to their primary deity, Teshub; while in Greece, a violent thunderstorm meant that the weather god Zeus was throwing a thunderbolt tantrum.

As far back as 1800 B.C., Hindus in India counted on their weather god, Indra, who carried a lightning bolt, to command the weather from his perch atop a large white elephant. In Scandinavia, Norse god Thor protected farmers and serfs from weather disasters.

EARLY FORECASTS

Around 580 B.C., the philosopher Thales of Miletus is said to have issued the very first seasonal crop forecast based on past olive harvests. According to legend, Thales was so confident of his forecast that he reserved the use of all the olive presses in his area before the harvest and made a tidy profit leasing them back to farmers when the bumper crop arrived.

The first real effort to gather all known weather information into one place was accomplished by the philosopher Aristotle around 350 B.C. In his essay "Meteorologica" the philosopher correctly guessed that the Sun put large masses of air into motion, and that water vapor could condense into clouds. But Aristotle was hamstrung by his era's notion that everything was made of four elements: fire, water, air, and earth. His attempts to force those elements to agree with the realities of nature limited his investigations. The other fallacy of his time was the belief that the earth was the center of the universe, which made it impossible to correctly explain the origin of the seasons.

Naming a Science

Aristotle's largest contribution to weather science was the term "meteorology," which we still use today. The word comes from the Greek *meteoros*, which means "high in the sky." In Aristotle's day anything falling from or appearing in the sky (like rain or clouds) was called a meteor.

False Tales

Some people still depend on folklore for weather safety, but many of the beliefs that have been passed down through the generations are misconceptions. For instance, some still insist the major danger from a hurricane is the wind, when most victims actually die in storm-spawned flooding.

Aristotle's pupil Theophrastus picked up his teacher's work, writing a journal called *On Weather Signs* that noted how nature can often be used to forecast the weather. He also established a link between the weather and certain kinds of illnesses, and was the first person in recorded history to identify sunspots.

For the next 2,000 years, the science of meteorology went dormant. Without accurate instruments to predict developing weather conditions or even measure the basic elements, weather forecasters leaned on folklore or nature for advice on planting crops and avoiding weather disasters.

LEARNING TO PREDICT THE WEATHER

Evolution of a Science

Things started falling back into place in the sixteenth century when Nicolaus Copernicus appeared on the scene. In 1543 he presented the theory that the Sun, not Earth, was at the center of the universe. Although still incorrect, his theory at least made room for an explanation of the seasons, and he correctly deduced that Earth rotated on its axis once a day and made the long trip around the Sun once each year. This was a scandalous and shocking idea at the time, because it contradicted religious dogma and suggested that man was just a part of nature, instead of being superior to it.

Leonardo da Vinci was fascinated by the weather. He noticed that a ball of wool weighed more on a rainy day than on a dry one, and further experiments led to his invention of the hygrometer, a device to measure the amount of water suspended in the air. Da Vinci wasn't content to measure the air's water content; he also invented the anemometer, which measures wind speed.

Even though the air's moisture level and speed now could be measured, for most of the sixteenth century no one could tell you how hot it was, because there were no thermometers yet. Enter Galileo Galilei, who remedied the thermometer shortage in 1593.

Galileo called his invention a thermoscope. It consisted of a long-necked glass bottle that was placed, upside down, into a vessel containing water. When the bottle was heated slightly, usually by the warmth of the experimenter's hands, the air inside expanded and the water was pushed downward. When the bottle cooled, the air contracted and the water rose back up into the neck of the bottle. Unfortunately, the thermoscope had no degree markings and was useless for determining temperature, but it paved the way for the more accurate versions to come.

THE PRESSURE INTENSIFIES

Now one could tell how humid it was and how fast the wind was blowing, and could get a vague idea of the temperature. But what about the air pressure?

Evangelista Torricelli, a student of Galileo's, created the first mercury barometer to measure atmospheric pressure in 1644, completing the list of instruments needed to develop an accurate weather forecast.

Verifying a Vacuum

Aristotle's contention that "nature abhors a vacuum" could be debated but not tested until Torricelli created one inside his mercury barometer. Catholic Jesuits, alarmed by this breach of faith, theorized that the mercury was being held up by invisible threads. But by then there was no stopping the weather revolution.

A French mathematician, Blaise Pascal, theorized that if air had weight, it should exert less and less pressure the higher you went. In 1648 he convinced his brother-in-law, armed with one of Torricelli's barometers, to climb almost 5,000 feet up a mountain. Sure enough, the higher he went, the lower the mercury sank.

The first recorded weather observations in the New World were made by a minister named John Campanius Holm in 1644 and 1645. Some people consider Holm, who lived in the colony of New Sweden near Wilmington, Delaware, to be America's first weatherman. In fact the National Weather Service gives an award in his name to outstanding volunteer weather observers each year.

OPPOSING SCALES

Have you ever wondered why the United States uses a method of measuring temperature that's different from the one used by the rest of the world? Blame Daniel Gabriel Fahrenheit, a German instrument maker who, in 1714, came up with the temperature scale that bears his name. He based his system on the difference between the freezing point of water and his own body temperature. Sound arbitrary and confusing? Indeed.

Celsius Preferred

The Fahrenheit scale is considered antiquated by scientists, who use the Celsius scale instead and wish everyone else would too. Old habits die hard—it'll probably be some time yet before everyone's on the same page temperature-wise.

Not content to leave well enough alone, Swedish astronomer Anders Celsius proposed another method. He divided the freezing and boiling points of water into equal degrees, which he called the centesimal system. Celsius decided the boiling point of water would be 0°, and the freezing point would be 100°. That must not have made any more sense at that time than it does now, because after his death, the scale was turned upside down, creating the measuring system still used today.

In 1793, Englishman John Dalton wrote a book called *Meteorological Observations and Essays* in which he advanced the theory that rain is caused by a drop in temperature, not air pressure. Taking the next step, he realized in 1802 that temperature actually affects the amount of water vapor the air can hold, a concept now called relative humidity.

WEATHER AND WARS

When the Military Drove Forecasting

Looking back through the history of warfare, it's evident that weather has played no small part in effecting both victories and defeats. The winter of 1777–1778 was no exception, and General George Washington's Continental Army learned that the weather can be more deadly than any mortal enemy.

After being defeated by the British Army in two major conflicts, Washington's troops marched to Valley Forge, Pennsylvania, 25 miles northwest of Philadelphia, in December 1777. The army of about 11,000 men had little to eat and inadequate clothing, and lived in tents while they set to work building huts in which to weather the coming winter.

By all accounts, that winter was unusually severe. Conditions got so bad that Washington wrote at one point, "For some days past there has been little less than a famine in the camp.... Naked and starving as they are, we cannot enough admire the incomparable patience and fidelity of the soldiery, that they have not been, ere this, excited by their suffering to a general mutiny and desertion."

FORGING A VICTORY

Although a few soldiers did desert, the ones who stayed were fiercely loyal to Washington. By the spring of 1778, nearly a fourth of the soldiers had died of smallpox, typhoid fever, malnutrition, and exposure to the severe cold, but the remaining troops were hardened by the experience. In May 1778 word came of the new alliance between

France and the United States, and the worst was over. Valley Forge marked the turning point in the war, and soon Washington and his men were chasing the British from Philadelphia.

Across the Frozen Potomac

The winter of 1780 was one of the worst on record. On the coast of Delaware's Delmarva Peninsula, ice formations towered 20 feet high, and the Potomac River froze over so solidly that it was possible to walk across it.

The French helped save the day at Valley Forge, but ended up with problems of their own years later during Napoleon's invasion of Russia and one of the largest weather-assisted routs in history.

WEATHER: RUSSIA'S SECRET WEAPON

In 1812, Napoleon controlled nearly all of Europe and had set his sights on Russia as his next conquest. In June of that year he crossed the Russian border with 600,000 troops and more than 50,000 horses, planning to march all the way to Moscow, living off the land along the way. The Russians had other ideas: as they retreated before the advancing French horde, they burned fields and destroyed houses, leaving little for the French to eat. Dry, hot conditions prevailed all the way to Moscow, and upon arriving there on September 14, the exhausted French troops found the city all but abandoned, its supplies depleted and much of its shelter destroyed. More than

20,000 troops had died of disease and exhaustion on the way, but the worst still lay ahead: winter was coming.

In the middle of October, with no offer of surrender from the tsar, Napoleon finally ordered a retreat. He had waited too long. As the weary troops turned toward home, an early and unusually cold air mass descended over them, and the weakest soldiers began to die.

Germans versus Russians

The weather has been Russia's ally in repelling foreign invaders throughout recorded history. In 1242 the pope sent German Teutonic Knights to take control of Russia and convert its people to Roman Catholicism. But Russian troops were more accustomed to the severe winter conditions and defeated the Germans on the frozen channel between the Peipus and Pskov Lakes in what became known as the "massacre on the ice."

Suddenly the weather turned warmer again, and roads that had been frozen solid turned into muddy quagmires. Streams and rivers that had been solid ice were now raging torrents, slowing the retreating troops even more. Then as quickly as the warm weather had arrived, it was replaced by an even colder air mass, and thousands more died in the driving snow and subzero temperatures.

In early December, Napoleon's troops finally crossed back over the border into Poland, but of the 600,000 fighting men who had invaded Russia just six months earlier, fewer than 100,000 remained. Half a million people had died in the Russian winter's icy embrace.

WORLD WAR II

Weather's Important Role

From the very first battle marking America's involvement in World War II, weather played a major role. On November 26, 1941, a fleet of four aircraft carriers and several other ships under the command of Admiral Isoroku Yamamoto steamed away from Japan toward Oahu, Hawaii, twelve days and 4,000 miles away.

Most of the trip was very difficult, with high seas and cold, stormy winter weather, but the rough conditions helped the huge fleet avoid detection. When the ships finally anchored 220 miles north of Oahu on December 7, 1941, and prepared to launch a surprise attack on the US naval base at Pearl Harbor, America's entry into the war was certain.

THE ALLIES STRIKE BACK

For the next four months, most of the news coming from the Pacific theater was negative, with defeats at Bataan and Corregidor disheartening the American public and military alike. On April 18, 1942, commander Jimmy Doolittle and his squadron of sixteen B-25 bombers (still 200 miles from their intended launch point) took off from the deck of the brand new aircraft carrier USS *Hornet* and turned toward Tokyo, more than 700 miles away.

Forced to take off early after the fleet was sighted by a Japanese patrol boat, the B-25s lumbered off the deck of the USS *Hornet* in a light rain. The B-25s had been stripped of any unnecessary equipment in order to carry more fuel, but on the way to Japan, they encountered a 20-mile-per-hour headwind that accelerated their fuel consumption. Arriving over Tokyo, the Raiders loosed volleys of 500-pound bombs on war-industry targets and then turned north along the coast toward China, where they hoped to find refuge.

It soon became obvious that the bombers wouldn't have enough fuel to make it to the Chinese airfields due to the headwinds they had encountered earlier. The situation got even worse when they encountered fog over the East China Sea, followed by a hard rain. With visibility near zero, navigators were forced to rely on dead reckoning to chart their course.

Suddenly, the winds shifted and the bomber crews found themselves being propelled by a strong tailwind. Still unable to see through the storm and low on fuel, most of the planes were forced to ditch in the ocean. In the end all sixteen B-25s were lost, seven men were injured, and three were killed. Eight crew members were taken prisoner by the Japanese, and only four of them survived the war. But the raid not only gave American morale a huge boost after several crushing defeats, it also dealt a shattering blow to Japanese pride.

THE PLOESTI RAID

In the summer of 1943, Operation Tidal Wave was launched from a Libyan airfield against Nazi-held oil refineries in Ploesti, Romania. Once again the weather would have a marked influence on the outcome. To reach the target and return, the mission's 179 B-24 bombers would have to fly more than 2,400 miles in eighteen hours. The flight over the Mediterranean was uneventful, with beautiful weather and unlimited visibility. Then, on reaching land, the bombers encountered a bank of huge cumulus clouds over the 9,000-foot peaks of the

Pindus Mountains. Flying blindly through the clouds at 12,000 feet, the planes became separated into two groups, neither one aware of the position of the other.

Because one bomber group arrived over the target well in advance of the second, the late arrivals suffered heavy casualties since the Germans had been alerted to their presence. Although most of the planes were able to drop their bombs, many important targets were missed in the confusion. Of the 179 planes in the mission, only ninety-nine returned to base, and fifty-eight of the surviving planes suffered severe combat damage.

THE BEGINNING OF THE END

The end of the Third Reich began with the Allies' Operation Overlord, a culmination of years of planning that aimed for the invasion of Europe and the end of the Führer's stranglehold on the embattled continent. Under the command of General Dwight D. Eisenhower, five beaches along the coast of France near Normandy were chosen as landing sites, and thousands of troops that had been in training for the mission for up to two years were moved into position.

D-Day Weather

If Operation Overlord hadn't taken advantage of the temporary break in the weather on June 6, the invasion might never have happened. Just a few days later, one of the worst June storms in English Channel history pounded the beaches, lasting for a full five days. Artificial harbors that had been created by the invaders at critical landing zones were completely destroyed by gigantic waves.

But before the giant operation could begin, several conditions had to be met in order to boost its chances for success. Low tide should coincide with the breaking dawn, giving the Allies the maximum amount of beach to work with. There should be a rising full Moon to support airborne operations, and a minimum visibility of 3 miles so naval gunners could see their targets. Winds should not exceed 8 to 12 miles per hour onshore, or 13 to 18 miles per hour offshore. No more than 60 percent of the sky should be covered by clouds, and they could not be lower than 3,000 feet.

Given these stringent requirements, forecasters estimated that there might be only three days in the entire month of June that would be suitable. Finally, June 5 was chosen as D-day, but after the troop ships and landing craft were loaded with men and supplies on the fourth, a storm system moved in over England. With high winds whipping across the English Channel and clouds hovering only 500 feet above its churning waves, Eisenhower was forced to delay the invasion.

On the night of June 4, Eisenhower's chief meteorological adviser, James Stagg, informed him that there might be a temporary break in the weather on the sixth, and the general uttered the fateful words "Okay, we'll go," throwing the formidable Allied invasion machine into gear. Six thousand landing craft and other ships left British ports on their way toward France, along with the 822 gliders and other aircraft that would transport Allied soldiers behind enemy lines. The first wave would be followed by 13,000 bombers, sent in to soften Axis positions in advance of the invading forces. This time the weather cooperated, and although Allied losses were heavy, especially at well-defended Omaha Beach, the invaders soon controlled the coast of Normandy and began the long push toward Berlin.

THE FINAL COUNTDOWN

Just as weather had influenced the first major attack of World War II against US forces, Pearl Harbor, the atmosphere intervened again in the last one: the mission to drop the atomic bomb that ended the war with Japan. The job of ending the war was brought about not by the *Enola Gay*, the B-29 Superfortress that leveled Hiroshima, but by another B-29, the *Bockscar*, which bombed Nagasaki. Although the *Enola Gay*'s mission was aided by clear skies over its target, the *Bockscar* faced tougher conditions.

In fact the residents of Kokura, on the northeast corner of the Japanese island of Kyushu, had the weather to thank for sparing their lives on August 9, 1944, when the *Bockscar* took to the air. President Truman had offered to spare Japan further agony after Hiroshima's destruction three days earlier, but promised that "if they do not now accept our terms, they may expect a rain of ruin from the air the like of which has never been seen on this earth."

With no response from the emperor, Kokura was selected as the next primary target because of its automatic weapons factories. Two weather observation planes were dispatched to the city an hour before the scheduled bombing, since the bombardier would need a clear sightline to the target. Reports indicated there would be only a 30 percent cloud cover over Kokura, but when *Bockscar* arrived, the crew found the entire city socked in under a thick layer of clouds. Had the weather been more accommodating, the bomb would have no doubt killed a young Kokura college student named Tetsuya Fujita, who would later become famous for developing a tornado damage scale that still bears his name.

Frustrated, the crew turned toward their secondary target, Nagasaki, a major shipbuilding center. When they arrived, they found that it, too, was mostly buried under clouds. Against orders, the crew decided to bomb by radar rather than return to its base in Okinawa and attempt to land with a fully armed atomic bomb on board. In the last twenty seconds of the bombing run, the bombardier sighted the target through a break in the clouds and released the bomb. Fifty seconds later, at 11:02 a.m., the crew experienced a white-hot flash followed by a violent shock wave.

Five days after the attack, the Japanese announced their acceptance of the Allies' terms of unconditional surrender.

The weather has been at the center of many major turning points throughout recorded history, and has been the single constant in all of mankind's conflicts. In the near future it's quite possible that advances in weather-control technology will allow people to use weather as a weapon.

HAARP

Manipulating the Weather

In 1990 the United States Navy and Air Force, together with the University of Alaska and the Defense Advanced Research Projects Agency (DARPA), began a project to research the ionosphere. It is called the High Frequency Active Auroral Research Program (HAARP) and has become the target of conspiracy theories as well as genuine concern.

HAARP's research is intended to improve communications and navigation, but it's possible that their findings could have other uses. Some scientists cite the concept of "nonlinear processes," in which a relatively small input of energy can be magnified into a much larger transmission of power. As professor Gordon J.F. MacDonald put it when he was a member of the President's Council on Environmental Quality, "The key to geophysical warfare is the identification of environmental instabilities to which the addition of a small amount of energy would release vastly greater amounts of energy." This leads many analysts to believe that HAARP's ultimate purpose will be as a long-range particle beam weapon of mass destruction.

Weather Service in the Military

In its study entitled "Spacecast 2020," the Air Force predicts that the National Weather Service will be absorbed by the Department of Defense. According to the report, weather service personnel would become paramilitary operatives, "supporting the military mission as a civilian during peacetime, becoming active duty military personnel during war, contingency (and) national emergency."

HAARP is only one part of a long-term, large-scale military program that aims to control and manipulate the weather for tactical and strategic advantages. In a report entitled "Weather as a Force Multiplier: owning the Weather in 2025," the benefits of weather modification are detailed by the government. By manipulating fog and precipitation over an enemy's location, the report says, visibility could be degraded in the target area while enhanced over friendly forces. The growth of developing storms over enemy strongholds could be accelerated, and triggering more lightning strikes on enemy targets would provide a natural kind of firepower.

One of the first steps in any military campaign is to obtain air superiority over a battlefield, but the report goes one step further, asserting that space superiority will be essential in future wars. That includes the HAARP concept of manipulating the ionosphere to produce lensing effects, which would not only enhance communications between friendly forces but could be used to disrupt the enemy's capabilities.

But these artificial electromagnetic fields can have a more insidious effect. They might be used by terrorists or by dictatorial governments seeking to control the population. As well, they have uses in dealing with security. Electromagnetic systems can produce mild to severe disruption, including rendering its subjects disoriented. Given this, it's understandable that the military would be interested.

In other words, the same kind of focused electromagnetic energy created by HAARP is capable of disrupting mental processes. It may sound like the stuff of science fiction, but all indications are that HAARP is currently fully operational.

Until recently, mankind's attempts to manipulate the weather have shown very little success, but new technological tools may be changing that. As with any experiment involving multiple unknown variables, the results will be unpredictable. Let's hope they're not detrimental to the earth and its inhabitants as well.

THE DOPPLER RADAR

A Revolution in Weather Forecasting

In the mid-1930s, with the situation in Europe deteriorating rapidly, the director of Britain's Air Ministry asked Robert Watson-Watt, superintendent of a radio department at England's National Physical Laboratory, if there was some way to develop a "death ray" that could shoot down aircraft from a distance. The request resulted not in a death beam but in Watson-Watt's report "Detection and Location of Aircraft by Radio Methods," which detailed how certain radio waves might be reflected off aircraft and back to the origin point, revealing the planes' positions.

Watson-Watt's invention came to be called Radio Detection and Ranging, or radar, and by the beginning of World War II, the coast of England bristled with radar installations. On those early radar screens, radar echoes from large storms would often obscure the images of approaching planes, and large areas of rain would show up as a green fog. By the end of the war, both the Axis and the Allies would depend on radar just as military forces do today.

There must have been an "aha!" moment when meteorologists first saw those radar echoes. After all the guesswork and ground observations used in the past to track weather systems, here was a system that could actually see the weather systems in motion. Radar was a forecaster's dream come true. After the war, surplus radar systems were pressed into service by the US Weather Bureau to track weather systems. Further research led to more powerful radars, which the bureau began to install along the coastline in 1954 as part of a hurricane early warning system.

The surplus radar units served their purpose, but as the years went by and the systems aged, spare parts became scarce and breakdowns were more frequent. Additionally, the old radar units were unable to detect developing tornadoes or accurately measure rainfall amounts. It became obvious that something new was needed.

DAZZLING DOPPLER

In the 1960s, the US Weather Service began experimenting with Doppler radar, which was a big improvement over the older types. During the late 1970s and early 1980s, Doppler radar began to appear at a few television stations, and around that time NOAA and the Department of Commerce joined forces to produce a next-generation radar system—NEXRAD—that would greatly improve severe weather forecasting. NEXRAD used the Doppler effect to spot rotating weather systems that often indicate a tornado is forming.

What Is the Doppler Effect?

Named after the nineteenth-century Austrian mathematician and physicist Christian Andreas Doppler, the Doppler effect describes the change in wavelengths (of sound or light) between two objects as a result of motion. For example, the change in sound as a motorcycle approaches, then passes, a stationary observer demonstrates the Doppler effect.

Light waves were much too fast to experiment with in the nineteenth century, so in 1845 Christoph Hendrik Diederik Buys Ballot, a recent graduate of the Netherlands' Utrecht University, set out to debunk Doppler's theory with a real-world test using sound waves. Ballot put a group of trumpeters on a train that would pass by a group of listeners. As the train passed with the trumpeters blasting away, the listeners heard the din rising in frequency as the train approached and then dropping as it moved away. On the train, however, the trumpets' pitch stayed the same.

Instead of refuting Doppler's theory, Ballot's experiment proved that the frequency of light or sound depends on the speed of an object's movement in relation to the viewer. The word "frequency" refers to how fast the peaks and valleys of a sound or light wave are moving past an observer. Let's say you're standing at a station watching an approaching train. When the engineer sounds the horn, the pitch will seem to rise because the speed of the moving train as it comes toward you is added to the speed of those sound waves, meaning the sound waves are pressed closer and closer together as they arrive at your ear. Once the train passes, the distance between the wave peaks is farther apart because the speed of the train is subtracted from the speed of the sound waves, and so the horn seems to shift to a lower pitch.

Using the Doppler Effect to Study Storms

In Doppler radar, pulses of microwave radiation are used instead of sound waves, but the effect is the same. When a Doppler beam is aimed at a storm, the echoes that return are coded by color: areas of precipitation moving toward the radar are shown in one color, while areas moving away from the radar are displayed in another. The National Weather Service's Weather Surveillance Radar 1988 Doppler (WSR-88D) uses green to indicate rain that's approaching the radar, and paints receding showers in red. When the radar sees green and red in close proximity, it's a sign of rotation within the storm that can indicate a developing tornado.

Doppler radar can identify gust fronts and microbursts as well, something conventional weather radar can't do. Peering deep within storms, the Doppler beam can identify mesocyclones (rotating air masses inside a thunderstorm) swirling inside. This allows forecasters to discover a region that may spawn a tornado and give them much more time to alert those in its path. Because about 30 percent of mesocyclones generate tornadoes and 95 percent produce severe weather, Doppler radar has become a welcome addition to a forecaster's arsenal.

Demo

WEATHER AND CLIMATE

What's the Difference?

The study of long-range weather patterns is called climatology. Weather is what's happening locally in the atmosphere right now. Climate is the average, or accumulated, weather for a region over a period of time, including extreme conditions and their frequencies. The longer data is gathered for an area, the more accurately its climate can be measured and its future climate predicted.

Generally, it takes thirty years or more to develop a truly detailed climatological profile for a region. So, if you wanted to find out whether it was going to rain during your trip to Walt Disney World the next day, a climatologist probably couldn't help you. However, he might be able to tell you if the currently landlocked Mouse House might become a beachfront resort in the future.

What Is the Greenhouse Effect?

A greenhouse protects plants by trapping solar energy during cold weather. Because only a small fraction of the Sun's heat ever reaches Earth, the atmosphere acts in much the same way to sustain life. If not for the atmosphere's heat-absorbing effects, the planet's average temperature would hover around –30°F.

In examining these global patterns, meteorologists have been able to categorize Earth's climates and group them into zones that share similar features. For instance, the Sahara desert in Africa is nowhere near California's Mojave Desert, yet both share many characteristics. You may tend to think of climates as encompassing huge areas of the earth's surface, but climates can be as small as a few hundred square feet. Such tiny areas of averaged weather are called microclimates, while weather conditions in areas from a few acres to several square miles fall into the category of a mesoclimate. The next step up is the climate of a whole state or country—a macroclimate; the average climate over the entire globe is called the global climate.

Studies have shown that the global climate is indeed changing, and some feel it's the fault of industries and automobiles that continue to pump huge quantities of particles into the atmosphere. It was once thought that the atmosphere was so vast that nothing could affect it, but it's now understood that it is actually very fragile. Views from orbit show the atmosphere as an impossibly thin, hazy blue line against the background of space. In fact if you could shrink the earth down to the size of a beach ball, the atmosphere would be about as thin as a human hair.

WHAT'S THE ATMOSPHERE?

The Air Up There

Earth's atmosphere is composed mostly of oxygen and nitrogen, with some carbon dioxide and other trace gases like argon and hydrogen thrown in for variety. Meteorologists divide the atmosphere into several layers, each of which blends seamlessly into the next. Nitrogen makes up around 78 percent of the air we breathe at the surface, with oxygen taking up about 21 percent. Unless you're an astronaut, you spend most of your time in the bottom layer of the atmosphere, called the troposphere, which extends anywhere from 5 to 10 miles up depending on how much of the Sun's energy is reaching the earth at the time.

THE TROPOSPHERE

In the troposphere, the temperature falls an average of 4°F for every 1,000 feet you climb, a phenomenon called the lapse rate. Eventually the temperature stops falling, meaning you've reached the tropopause and the beginning of the next layer, the stratosphere. Really, you wouldn't want the temperature to fall much lower anyway: at the tropopause, it can dip as low as –70°F. You'd think the temperature would just keep on falling as you leave the troposphere and gain more altitude, but that's not the case.

THE STRATOSPHERE

Instead, as you climb up into the stratosphere, the temperature begins to rise again, up to a high of around 40°F. One reason for that is because the stratosphere contains the ozone layer, which acts as a protective blanket to prevent harmful amounts of ultraviolet (UV) solar radiation from reaching the earth's surface (and the people on it) and helps to warm the stratosphere. Even where the amount of ozone is greatest—around 16 miles up—you'll find only about twelve ozone molecules for every million molecules of air, but that's still enough to block out the worst of the UV rays. That's a good thing, because UV radiation is known to cause skin cancer, and can even induce genetic mutations in DNA.

Climbing even higher, you finally reach the edge of the stratosphere, or stratopause, at around 30 miles above the earth's surface. Now you're really getting into nosebleed territory: at this height, the air is much too thin to breathe, and atmospheric pressure is only about one millibar (the metric equivalent to mercury). By contrast, air pressure at sea level is about 1,013 millibars. You're now above most of the atmosphere.

THE MESOSPHERE

The mesosphere is the next layer, extending from 30–50 miles high. With very little ozone to provide warmth, the temperature begins to fall again, to a low of about –130°F. It continues to decrease until you reach the mesopause, then begins to rise again as you enter the thermosphere, which extends from 50 to more than 120 miles above the earth.

THE HOT ZONE

Perhaps "rise" isn't the right word—temperatures in the thermosphere can reach a blistering 2,700°F. The thermosphere gets that hot because it's the first layer of air the Sun's rays hit as they zoom toward Earth. A space shuttle must pass through the thermosphere on its way to and from orbit, so the obvious question is: why doesn't it burn up? Fortunately, at that height there are so few air molecules that the net amount of heat energy hitting the shuttle isn't enough to destroy it.

Why Don't All Meteorites Burn Up in the Atmosphere?

Some are just too big or dense for the thermosphere to handle. Thousands of rocks from the size of pebbles down to grains of sand burn up each day, but space rocks larger than about 33 feet in diameter can usually make it to the ground (most often in pieces).

The lack of air molecules would actually make it feel downright cold if you could somehow sit out in the thermosphere for a few moments. It sounds crazy, but there just wouldn't be enough air molecules to heat up your skin. It's a good thing for us that the number of molecules in the thermosphere is still great enough to intercept and destroy most incoming meteorites, however.

The thermosphere also contains most of the ionosphere, so-called because energy from the Sun smacks into molecules at that height and separates them into ions, which carry a positive charge, and free electrons, which are negatively charged. Many years ago, it was discovered that this layer reflects radio waves, especially at night, allowing the transmission of signals beyond the curvature of the earth for hundreds of miles or more. This principle allows ham radio operators to receive broadcasts from faraway countries, although the effect is not always predictable.

A Planet Gone Wrong

As an example of uncontrolled warming, scientists point to Venus, a planet nearly the same size as Earth but with a much more hostile atmosphere. On Venus the "air" is about 96 percent carbon dioxide with a temperature hot enough to melt lead. Scientists say the same conditions may occur on Earth if pollution isn't controlled.

What lies above the thermosphere? If you think the answer is air, think again. The layer above 120 miles of altitude—the exosphere—contains so few molecules that many of them are actually able to escape Earth's gravity and fly off into space. The exosphere is the domain of satellites and space shuttles, a transitional zone between Earth's atmosphere and interplanetary space. The exosphere has no real upper boundary; it just becomes more and more diffuse until it's no longer detectable.

THE WATER CYCLE

It's Raining

Most of the moisture in the atmosphere—about 90 percent—comes from the oceans. Water is constantly recycled from the ocean into the air and back through a process called the water cycle. At any one time, the oceans contain about 97 percent of the earth's water; the atmosphere contains only about 0.001 percent. Landmasses and ice hold the remainder. Still, if that seemingly tiny amount of atmospheric water vapor suddenly turned into rain, it would cover the entire Earth with an inch of water.

About 121,000 cubic miles of water evaporate from the earth's surface each year, with around 86 percent of that coming from the oceans. The evaporation occurs due to the Sun's heating of the sea surface. Warm air can hold a lot of moisture (think of steam), so some of the ocean surface converts to water vapor and is drawn up into the air.

Water As Coolant

Water can absorb a lot of heat before it begins to heat up itself. That's why water makes such a good coolant for automobile radiators and why oceans prevent abrupt seasonal changes. Instead, winter comes on gradually as oceans slowly release their stored heat into the atmosphere, and summer takes a while to set in as the sea begins to reabsorb heat.

Evaporation occurs anywhere there is water, from lakes and rivers to storm drains and birdbaths. Plants even give off water through a process called transpiration, as they ooze small droplets of moisture from the undersides of their leaves. All of this warm water vapor begins to rise, joining billions of other water molecules in a dizzying ascent into the troposphere.

WHAT GOES UP MUST COME DOWN

Eventually the vapor reaches cooler layers and condenses around small particles of dust, pollen, or pollution. As the condensation process continues, the droplets become too big for the wind to support and they begin a plunge toward the surface. Not all the precipitation reaches the ground, however; some of it evaporates directly back into the atmosphere on its way down. What's left finally reaches the ground in the form of rain, snow, hail, or sleet, sometimes ruining picnics or closing schools in the process.

If the precipitation falls in the ocean, the cycle is ready to begin again right away, and that's exactly what happens to the majority of raindrops and snowflakes. After all, oceans cover more than 70 percent of the earth's surface, making them a big target. When it rains or snows over land, however, the cycle takes a little more time to complete.

Most water reaching the land surface runs off into ditches and streams where it finds its way back into lakes or the ocean. But some water seeps into the ground, percolating down until it is either trapped or it encounters a horizontal flow deep under the surface. The seeping water goes with the flow until it encounters a large underground reservoir known as an aquifer. Most aquifers eventually drain off into streams, which carry the water to rivers and canals and back to the sea. Then, of course, the whole cycle begins anew.

THE THREE LEVELS OF CLOUDS

Water in the Air

The air in the upper troposphere, the bottom layer of the atmosphere, is very dry and cold, so water vapor at high altitudes can't remain in a liquid state for long. Clouds that form there are made of ice crystals and are usually very wispy. High clouds appear white because they're not thick enough to block the Sun. Cirrus is the most common type of cloud found at these rarified heights of 20,000 to 60,000 feet.

You might think a cirrus cloud's upturned "tail" points in the direction of the prevailing wind, but the opposite is true. As the ice crystals that form the tail begin to fall, they encounter a level where wind speed or direction suddenly changes, and the cloud gets pulled like taffy (or cotton candy) into a long, thin streamer.

Mare's Tails

Sometimes known as mare's tails, cirrus clouds often resemble thin filaments of white hair being stretched out by high-level winds. Cirrus clouds generally move from west to east and often predict an approaching low-pressure system, which is a good hint to go find an umbrella.

Cirrus clouds can spread out until they cover the entire sky, forming a thin layer called cirrostratus. You can see right through cirrostratus clouds, and because they're composed of ice crystals, you'll often see a halo where the Sun or Moon peeks through this wispy veil. Because they often form in advance of an approaching cold front or storm, cirrostratus can mean rain in the next twelve to twenty-four hours.

One of the most beautiful cloud types is cirrocumulus, which forms a series of small rounded patches or puffs that often extend across the sky in long rows. Because of their regular, repetitive pattern, cirrocumulus clouds can resemble the scales of a fish, which is why a sky full of cirrocumulus is also called a mackerel sky.

STUCK IN THE MIDDLE

Forming at an altitude of 6,500–26,000 feet, clouds in the troposphere's middle levels can be composed of either water or ice, or a combination of the two. Midlevel cloud types are easy to remember because the most common ones always begin with the prefix *alto-*. The two main middle cloud types are altocumulus and altostratus.

Altostratus clouds are either gray or blue-gray, are often thick enough to blot out the Sun, and can blanket hundreds of miles of sky. Sometimes altostratus does allow a glimpse of the Sun, but it's a dim view, like looking through tracing paper. Altostratus clouds are often confused with cirrostratus, but there's an easy way to tell them apart: if you look at the ground and don't see a shadow, it's probably altostratus. Also, altostratus clouds don't produce halos. This type of cloud often means you're in for an extended, steady rain in the near future.

Altocumulus clouds have a distinctive patchy or puffy pattern like cirrocumulus. They're composed mostly of water rather than ice, though, so they often appear gray instead of white. The individual puffs are also larger than cirrocumulus and sometimes form little cottony "castles" in the sky, meaning it won't be long before it will probably—guess what—rain!

THE REAL LOWDOWN

Low-level clouds, stratus clouds, form below 6,500 feet, and at that height are almost always made of water droplets unless it's winter. Stratus clouds are arguably the most boring clouds in existence; they usually cover the whole sky in a uniform gray cloak, sometimes completely blotting out the Sun. You won't generally see much rain falling from stratus clouds, although they can produce some light drizzle or mist. They usually form during stable atmospheric conditions when a large, moist air mass rises slowly to a level where it can condense.

On the other hand, nimbostratus is a dark gray cloud that forms when a front of warm, moist air meets a mass of relatively cool air. When you're under a nimbostratus layer, you often can't even see the cloud itself because of the rain and the thick mist formed by evaporation. If the air becomes saturated enough, another layer of ragged, swift clouds called scud can form below the nimbostratus. When you see this type of cloud coming, you might as well settle in with a good book or find an old movie marathon on TV, because it's probably going to rain or snow for quite a while.

Stratocumulus clouds are similar to altocumulus, but they're found at lower altitudes and their individual cells are bigger. They don't produce much rain and often form when cumulus clouds spread out across the sky and begin to merge. Stratocumulus clouds generally appear in patches, and you can often see blue sky between them.

From Fair to Middling—to Monster

Cumulus clouds are often thought of as fair-weather clouds, and they usually are—but they can grow into something far more ominous. Cumulus clouds look like big balls of white or light gray cotton drifting across the sky, usually have a flat base, and don't generate much precipitation in their young, puffy phase. They most often form when the morning Sun heats up the earth's surface and fills the sky with hundreds of popcornlike clouds floating serenely over your head.

As the day progresses and it gets hotter, cumulus clouds can begin to blossom upward, now resembling a cauliflower more than a cotton ball. Called cumulus congestus, these towering pillars of water vapor are the raw material of the most dangerous cloud of all—the cumulonimbus.

As the 300-pound gorilla of the cloud kingdom, cumulonimbus gets a lot of respect. These are the giant thunderstorm clouds that can produce lightning, hailstorms, and tornadoes. On color weather radar, cumulonimbus cells glow bright red, a warning that their tops have grown high into the atmosphere and severe weather is on its way. Violent updrafts within the storm, which can reach speeds of 100 miles per hour or more, keep it growing ever higher into the troposphere. If the monster cloud has enough energy, it will continue upward until reaching the tropopause or even break through to the stratosphere, where it will begin to flatten and form an anvil shape.

Cumulonimbus can also become nurseries for other types of clouds. When a thunderstorm grows all the way up to the troposphere, it's in cirrus territory. The tops or anvils of cumulonimbus can shear off and become cirrus or cirrostratus clouds, and are often swept hundreds of miles downwind to become an early warning of approaching storms.

How Low Can They Go?

Nimbostratus is included in the low-level cloud category because thunderstorms always begin near the earth's surface. But the winner in the lowest-cloud-ever category has to be fog, which is a cloud that forms right at ground level. Actually, fog is nothing more than a stratus cloud you can walk through.

Acid Fog

Fog that forms near sources of pollution (like industrial cities) tends to be thicker than ordinary fog since it contains so many more small particles for the water vapor to bond with. Unfortunately, these particles often include noxious chemicals that create acid fog, a concoction that can cause serious respiratory distress and other health problems.

Fog usually forms at night when a low layer of moist air is cooled by the ground, creating a surface cloud called radiation fog (caused by cool air radiating from the surface). A light breeze can actually cause the fog to become thicker, as it brings more warm air in contact with the cooler ground. Since warm air rises and cool air falls, you'll most often find the heaviest fog in the lowest-lying areas, especially near sources of moisture like lakes and streams. Fog can hang around long after the Sun comes up, because evaporation of the dew that formed the night before adds even more moisture to the air, replacing the fog that has burned off as the morning Sun warms the ground.

Of course, fog doesn't really burn—if it did, San Francisco would have been a cinder a long time ago. Rather, the Sun's light and heat eventually penetrate the upper, middle, and finally the lower layers of a fog bank, causing more and more evaporation until the fog is gone.

HOW TO BUILD A CLOUD

Use Dirt and Water

Although there's usually plenty of water vapor in the atmosphere, it could never condense without the presence of tiny particles—called condensation nuclei—because of the high surface tension of each vapor droplet. Condensation nuclei are so small that a volume of air the size of your index finger contains anywhere from 1,000 to 150,000 of them, but they make the perfect seed for a cloud droplet. Some of these specks, such as salt particles, bond easily with vapor and are called hygroscopic, or water seeking. Ever notice how difficult it is to get salt out of a shaker when the air is humid? Those salt particles love their moisture. On the other hand, other atmospheric bits are hydrophobic, or water repelling, like particles from petroleum by-products, and resist binding with water vapor even when the humidity is more than 100 percent.

So now you know a cloud's dirty little secret. Put condensation nuclei and water vapor together, and voilà—instant cloud, right? Well, as usual, there's a bit more to it than that. You also have to have air that's (a) rising; (b) expanding; and (c) cooling.

BOILING UP A CLOUD

If you've ever watched a pot of spaghetti cooking, you've probably noticed that it seems to circulate in the pot even if you don't stir it. Through a process called convection, the hot water carries the spaghetti toward the surface. When it cools slightly, more hot water rises to take its place, circulating the noodles over and over.

With cloud formation, the Sun heats the earth's surface, causing it to radiate warmth. Any area that heats more rapidly than its surroundings, such as deserts or large areas of asphalt or concrete, can create a bubble of warm air that rises into the sky, mixing with the cooler, drier air around it. When this happens, the warm air expands and cools, and if this process continues, the air bubble will begin to fall back toward the surface again, just like spaghetti circulating in the pot. But if more warm air arrives from underneath, it will keep growing until it reaches the saturation point and condenses, making a fluffy little cumulus cloud.

When the cloud gets big enough to cast a sizable shadow, it starts to cut off its own heat engine as the ground below it cools. This throws a monkey wrench into the whole convection process, and the cloud begins to show ragged edges as the wind moves it along, causing it to eventually dissipate. But now the ground is free to heat up again, and soon another bubble floats skyward, ready to make yet another cumulus cloud. That's why you'll often see one cloud after another form around the same spot on a sunny afternoon.

Equilibrium and Instability

Of course, when the atmosphere is unstable, even more interesting things can happen. When meteorologists use the word *stable*, they're talking about the atmosphere being in balance. Air that's in a state of balance, or equilibrium, holds true to Newton's First Law of Motion: when it's at rest, it tends to remain at rest, and so it resists any upward or downward movement. In other words, it doesn't like to be pushed around. So if an air mass encounters surrounding air that's cooler or warmer, and quickly adapts to that temperature, the air mass is said to be stable.

On the other hand, the atmosphere becomes unstable when there's a big difference in temperature between the upper and lower layers, or between warm and cold air masses. Generally speaking, a rising air mass will become unstable. Because warm air rises, instability usually results from the warming of surface air. If air at ground level is warm and moist and upper levels are cold and dry, a process called convective instability can occur, causing a rapid, often violent, cloud growth that can produce severe thunderstorms and tornadoes quicker than you can say, "Run for the basement!"

Growing Pains

Let's take a closer look at a cumulus cloud as it grows up to become a towering cumulonimbus. We've discussed how cumulus clouds form and dissipate in a stable environment, but when the air above is cooler than the layers below, more and more heat is released inside the cloud as it rises and its vapor condenses. Rain droplets and ice particles begin to form and are churned and swirled by the turbulence from the rising air. Strong updrafts form in the cloud's core, causing it to grow even faster. The rain and ice particles surge upward, getting larger and larger as they merge with other specks of moisture, creating a swirling mass of rain and ice within the cloud. And even with all this activity, no rain is falling yet, because the cloud is putting all its energy into the growth stage.

Constant Storms

There are nearly 1,800 thunderstorms occurring worldwide at any moment, although most last an average of only thirty minutes. Out of the 100,000 or so storms that occur each year in the United States, only about 10 percent are classified as severe, but even small storms can create heavy rain and dangerous lightning.

In the next phase, called the mature stage, the raindrops and ice crystals get too large to be supported by the updraft and so they start to fall. This creates downdrafts within the cloud, and a pitched battle between falling and rising air begins. With updrafts still raging at speeds of up to 6,000 feet per minute, the severe turbulence causes a tremendous amount of friction in the cloud, and jagged lightning bolts begin to stab outward and downward as the storm mushrooms up toward the stratosphere. As the rain-cooled downdrafts reach the ground, they spread out horizontally into a gust front. Rain and hail begin to hammer cars, trees, buildings, and anything else unlucky enough to be caught in the storm's path. The monster cloud's top reaches the jet stream, and strong winds begin to pull it into a long anvil shape.

As the gust front spreads out underneath the storm, it cuts off the cloud's supply of warm air. Eventually, the storm's downward-moving air currents gain the upper hand, and the cloud's growth slows and finally stops. Soon the internal updrafts cease completely, and downdrafts are all that's left, carrying the rest of the cloud's moisture to the ground as rain, often for several more hours.

Super-Sized Storms

If thunderstorms are the 300-pound gorilla of weather, supercells are the King Kongs. Although fewer than one in eighty thunderstorms develop into supercells, the ones that do are extremely dangerous and can be unpredictable. Supercells are the storms that most often produce tornadoes, making them the targets of storm chasers during springtime on the Great Plains.

Supercells feed off wind shear, which is the effect caused by winds blowing in different directions and speeds at different atmospheric levels. Wind shear actually tilts the storm, causing the cooler air descending inside to be pushed completely out of the cloud. Warm moist air is still free to surge in, however, and without the cooler air to act as a stabilizer, the storm's consumption of warm air becomes a feeding frenzy, creating a strong, rotating updraft within the storm called a mesocyclone—the first stage of a tornado.

Because of the strong vertical wind shear inside a developing supercell (where updrafts can reach speeds of 150 miles an hour!), the updrafts and downdrafts can actually wrap around each other, creating an extremely volatile environment. These violent currents can keep hail suspended for so long that it can reach the size of grapefruit or larger before finally escaping the storm and plummeting to earth.

The National Weather Service gives supercells special attention, using radar to peer deep into their cores to catch early signs of developing tornadoes, which cause a characteristic "hook echo." When a severe thunderstorm or tornado warning is given for your area, believe it and take cover as soon as possible.

HAIL AND SNOW

Damaging and Dangerous

Most people enjoy watching a good snowfall. After all, there's nothing like sitting around a fireplace with a cup of cocoa, watching through the window as the landscape is transformed into a beautiful white blanket. And many people like the excitement of a hailstorm—the thud of hailstones as they hit the ground. Unfortunately, both forms of precipitation have the potential to cause a good deal of damage and even death.

HAIL

While heavy rain can limit visibility and soak you to the skin, a hailstorm is capable of breaking windshields, decimating crops, and even injuring livestock. If it wasn't for updrafts, hail would never grow very large, and golf ball–sized and larger specimens would be unheard of. But as ice particles fall through a cumulonimbus cloud, they inevitably encounter strong vertical winds and get swirled skyward again, picking up extra layers of supercooled water droplets as they zoom above the freezing level.

If the updrafts are strong enough, like those in a supercell, the developing hailstones ride a wild roller coaster of wind as they spin up and around inside the storm, growing larger by the minute. Finally some become so big that they overcome the updraft's power and begin to drop toward the ground. Falling at speeds of up to 120 miles an hour, they can dent cars and destroy crops, raising insurance rates wherever they strike.

Size May Vary

Most hail is relatively small—around 2 inches in diameter or less—but on July 23, 2010, the great-granddaddy of all hailstones fell on Vivian, South Dakota. The hailstones measured 8 inches in diameter and weighed almost 2 pounds. Never mind an umbrella—with hail that size, you'd need a bomb shelter.

If you cut a hailstone in half, you can see the multiple layers of ice that mark its journey through the thunderstorm. Generally, the larger the hailstone, the more severe the updrafts were in the storm that it came from.

SNOW

Snow forms from tiny particles of ice suspended in clouds up above the freezing level. As the particles form, they arrange themselves into hexagonal shapes due to the molecular structure of water, which is why simple snow crystals always have six points. Snowflakes that fall through a layer of slightly warmer air, however, can bind with other flakes to form very large, intricate structures that look like beautiful silver jewelry under a microscope.

Much of the rain that falls in the summer actually begins as snow and ice high in the tops of cumulonimbus clouds. In the wintertime the freezing level is much lower, and if you live in a snow-prone region, you're aware that snowflakes can easily make it all the way to the ground, where they gather with billions of their friends for an impromptu party on your lawn.

Snow flurries usually fall from cumulus clouds and provide a light dusting of crystals that don't cause much trouble for those below. Snow squalls, on the other hand, are brief but very intense snowstorms that are the equivalent of a summer downpour. They arrive with little warning, and their intense driving winds often create near-whiteout conditions in a matter of minutes.

Whiteouts

A whiteout occurs when the clouds from which snow is falling take on a bright, uniformly white appearance. This happens when the light reflected off the snow is about the same as the light coming through the clouds, making objects in the storm very difficult to see.

Not Your Average Snowstorm

Wind-driven snow officially becomes a blizzard when below-freezing temperatures are accompanied by winds of more than 35 miles per hour and visibility down to a quarter mile or less. In a severe blizzard, winds exceed 45 miles per hour and temperatures plunge to 10°F or lower. Blizzards can pile snow into gigantic drifts that can make travel impossible. During the great blizzard of 1888, known as the Great White Hurricane, some snowdrifts were measured as high as 50 feet.

The 1888 blizzard actually led directly to the creation of the New York subway system, as city leaders vowed to prevent the weather from ever bringing the city to such a standstill again. The entire East Coast, from Maine to the Chesapeake Bay, buried in up to 50 inches of snow, was cut off from the rest of the world as telegraph and telephone wires snapped like twigs under the crushing weight of snow and ice. Washington, New York, Philadelphia, and Boston were paralyzed for days. At least 100 sailors were lost at sea, 200 ships ran aground, and, with lifesaving water frozen in pipes and hydrants, raging fires caused more than $25 million in property losses. More than 400 people perished in what became known as the worst snowstorm in American history.

What Is a Frontal Passage?

A frontal passage is the movement of the boundary between two air masses over a particular location. Frontal passages are usually accompanied by a change in wind speed and direction, humidity, cloud cover, precipitation, and temperature.

If you follow winter weather on TV, you've probably noticed that cities like Buffalo and Syracuse, New York, seem to get more than their share of snow. This is due to the "lake effect," a condition that occurs when cold air moves over a warmer body of water, in this case the Great Lakes. Unlike the Great Plains, where snowstorms usually move through, release their quota of snow and leave, states to the south and east of the Great Lakes are often dumped on for days after a frontal passage, as cold air flowing south and east over the lakes picks up moisture and warmth from the water's surface and carries it shoreward.

Snow Wonder

As damaging as snow can be, however, it has a gentler side. Since snow doesn't conduct heat very well, dry snow can actually act as an insulator, protecting plants below its surface by preventing the ground from losing all of its warmth. Just as air spaces within a down jacket help insulate you from the cold, tiny gaps between dry snowflakes act as buffer zones against the cold air above. This same effect is what causes snow to absorb sound, making a walk through the woods after a snowfall a quiet, mesmerizing experience.

Warm Great Lakes

The Great Lakes, due to their size and depth, are able to retain much of their summer warmth well into fall and winter. When an air mass warmed by its passage over a lake reaches the shore, it is forced to rise rapidly—a process called orographic lifting—and heavy snow and snow squalls are often the result.

Have you ever heard someone say that it's "too cold to snow"? Is it really possible for the temperature to drop so low that snow can no longer form? Well, no. It's true that there may be a lack of snow on cold, still evenings, when high pressure drives away any snow-producing clouds. But while it's true that cold, dry air can't hold as much moisture as warmer air, there is always at least some water vapor present, and where there's vapor, there can be precipitation.

On the flip side, you may have seen snow fall when the temperature at ground level is above freezing. For this to happen, the air aloft must be very dry. As snow begins to fall from clouds above the freezing level, it encounters warmer layers of the atmosphere and starts to melt. But because the air is dry, the melting snow evaporates quickly, cooling the air and making it possible for more flakes to penetrate downward. Eventually some of these flakes can make it to the surface, although they won't last very long in a frozen state.

THE POLAR VORTEX

Precipitating Bigger Snowstorms

In the winter of 2015, the northeastern United States received an unprecedented amount of snow and freezing temperatures. Boston, in many ways at the epicenter of the event, received a record-breaking 110 inches of snow (the previous record had been 107). Strong storms pummeled various parts of the country: in Colorado, at Wolf Creek Pass, which crosses the Continental Divide, 23 inches of snow came down within twenty-four hours. At the same time, temperatures plummeted: Whiteface Mountain, part of the Adirondack Mountains in New York State, measured a record –114°F. New England was battered in February by a series of Nor'easters that piled snowdrift upon snowdrift.

A Nor'easter

Nor'easters can do some real damage when a high-pressure system over New England or the northern Atlantic blocks the northern progression of a low-pressure system. As the low stops moving, its counterclockwise winds meet the clockwise gusts of the high-pressure system, battering the coastline with severe winds.

A Nor'easter storm, which begins as a low-pressure system over warm Gulf Stream waters, forms off the East Coast of the United States and moves northward into New England. These storms usually form between October and April, and as they move up the coast and encounter frigid arctic air flowing down from Canada, instability increases and the chance for heavy snow and gale-force winds is great. Most Nor'easters don't turn into major storms, but the ones that do, such as those of 2015, live in memory and folklore for generations.

As the severe winter continued across the country, nightly television viewers were increasingly treated to comments about a "polar vortex."

WHAT THE HECK IS A POLAR VORTEX?

A polar vortex refers to an area of low pressure that forms near one of the poles. At the North Pole it rotates counterclockwise; at the South Pole, clockwise. Polar vortices are normally more active in the south than in the north, but 2015 presented a meteorological anomaly. The vortex probably caused temperatures across much of the northern part of the country to drop anywhere between 15°F and 35°F.

In practical terms, this meant that very little of the heavy snowfall that came down across the Northeast and Upper Midwest had a chance to melt. Instead, it piled up, defying efforts to clear it.

An additional feature of polar vortices is that they tend to deplete the ozone layer, since their chemical composition creates chlorine, a gas that causes the ozone layer to dissolve. This has created a hole in the ozone layer near the South Pole.

The strength of vortices can be increased by volcanic eruptions or by El Niño (for details, see the section dedicated to El Niño). The latter is probably responsible for the intensified northern polar vortex in the winter of 2014–2015, which brought so much misery to those living in the northern parts of the United States.

SLEET OR FREEZING RAIN?

There Is a Difference

If descending, partially melted snowflakes or raindrops fall through a colder layer near the ground, they can refreeze into sleet, which is tiny clear or translucent ice pellets that sound like falling rice when they hit your window.

When the layer of colder surface air is shallow, raindrops falling through it won't have time to freeze and will hit the surface as freezing rain, which spreads out into a thin film of ice as soon as it hits any cold surface. While sleet is relatively harmless, ice storms caused by freezing rain can be killers, as roads become slick with ice, causing auto accidents and bringing even foot traffic to a standstill. Freezing rain can create winter wonderlands by coating trees with a twinkling, crystalline glaze, but it can also bring down telephone and power lines, cutting off communications and creating severe electrocution hazards.

Aren't Sleet and Hail the Same Thing?

Sleet can form only when the weather is very cold, while hail is a warm-weather phenomenon based on heat convection. Hail forms while bouncing around in a thunderstorm, while sleet is created when a snowflake or raindrop refreezes during a winter storm.

Aircraft are especially vulnerable to ice, which in a freezing rain can build up very quickly and is very difficult to remove. A coating of ice on a plane's wings increases its weight, which makes it more difficult to gain altitude at takeoff. Moreover, the ice disturbs the airflow over the wings and fuselage, which makes it more difficult for the plane to stay airborne. Airports in ice-prone areas maintain de-icing crews, who spray aircraft with an antifreeze mixture designed to melt ice before it can accumulate to dangerous levels.

The National Center for Atmospheric Research (NCAR) has found that the most dangerous icing forms when planes fly through supercooled drizzle in clouds. Although the drops are small, they freeze quickly and form a rough ice layer called rime that decreases lift and increases drag much more than a layer of smooth ice would. The National Weather Service's Aviation Weather Center in Kansas City, Missouri, is using supercomputers to develop forecast maps that will enable pilots to steer clear of icy drizzle while aloft.

Down at ground level, however, even a good forecast isn't always enough to protect people and property from the dangers of an ice storm. In January of 1998 a severe ice storm hit the northeastern United States and Canada, causing forty-four deaths. In some places more than 3 inches of freezing rain fell, coating trees, buildings, and cars with ice that was more than an inch thick. In the aftermath 500,000 people were without power in the United States, including more than 80 percent of the population of Maine. Things were even worse in Canada, where more than three million people lost electricity. Damage estimates for both countries totaled $4.5 billion.

HIGH PRESSURE AND LOW PRESSURE

It's Windy Outside

To understand why air moves, it helps to understand air pressure, which is the amount of force that moving air exerts on an object. There are several ways of measuring atmospheric pressure, the most common being inches of mercury, which we use in the United States, and millibars, the metric equivalent.

If you could somehow isolate a 1-inch-square column of the atmosphere, from the surface all the way to the top of the troposphere, it would weigh just about 14.7 pounds. So meteorologists say that air pressure at sea level is 14.7 pounds per square inch, or psi. That translates to 29.92 inches of mercury (abbreviated as Hg, the symbol for mercury on the periodic table of elements) or 1013.25 millibars. In case you're wondering, one millibar is equal to 0.02953 inches of mercury.

With nearly 15 pounds of pressure pushing against every square inch of your body, you'd think it would be hard to even take a breath. Fortunately, nature does its best to stay in balance, and there is just as much pressure pushing outward in each cell of your body as there is outside pushing inward. This shows you just how well we've adapted to living on the surface of this planet. But what if you're not on the surface, but up higher where air pressure is less, as you find when climbing a mountain or flying in a plane? As you climb higher, the pressure in your body becomes greater than the pressure outside, and you'll probably start to notice an uncomfortable pressure in your inner ear as those 14.7 pounds of pressure try to get out.

WEIGHING THE AIR

Atmospheric pressure is measured using a device called a barometer, which is either liquid filled (which is where the inches-of-mercury method comes from) or metal based. Although you'll hear your local TV weatherperson use the term "inches of mercury" a lot, liquid barometers are rarely used these days; the aneroid barometer, which uses variations in the shape of a metal cell to measure air pressure, is now much more common, as are newer electronic models.

Unlike temperature, air pressure decreases the higher you go in the atmosphere. (You'd think temperature would go down with increases in altitude, and it does to a certain point. But then it goes up again before coming back down. It isn't what you'd expect, is it? For details, see the section titled What's the Atmosphere?) The only thing keeping all of Earth's air from leaking out into space is gravity, which pulls air molecules toward the earth's surface. Air at ground level is under more pressure because of the weight of all the air above it, so the higher you go, the less pressure you'll find. At a height of 3.5 miles, air pressure is only half what it is at the surface, so at this altitude you're above half of all the air molecules in the atmosphere.

HIGHS AND LOWS MAKE WIND

When warm air rises, it relieves the pressure of the air beneath it and so creates an area of low pressure. But if that same rising air mass cools, then it sinks and presses down on the air below it to create an area of high pressure. Because the atmosphere is always trying to keep itself in balance, and because low-pressure systems are actually partial vacuums, air moves from high-pressure systems to areas of low pressure, producing wind.

The difference in air pressure between air masses is called a pressure gradient, and the higher the gradient, the faster the winds will blow. Because the earth rotates, those winds turn to the right in the Northern Hemisphere and to the left in the Southern, following a path first discovered in 1835 by Gaspard-Gustave de Coriolis, a French engineer and mathematician. Coriolis applied the element of rotation to Newton's Laws of Motion, describing how a free-floating object near the earth's surface appears to curve as the globe rotates beneath it. You can duplicate the Coriolis effect by having someone turn a globe while you try to draw a straight line on it from north to south with a piece of chalk: what you'll end up with is a curved line.

PUTTING A SPIN ON THE WEATHER

The Coriolis effect is what imparts rotation to weather systems. It affects any moving object not attached to the earth's surface, from space shuttles to artillery shells.

You've probably seen weather maps with swirled lines that sometimes look like fingerprints. These swirled lines are called isobars, and they connect locations with equal air pressure. Multiple isobars usually form a target shape, and in the middle you'll find a capital "H" or "L"—a high- or low-pressure area. Because high-pressure areas contain air that is sinking toward the surface, they're usually associated with fair weather; while low-pressure systems, which contain rising air, are more unstable and often mean a dose of rain, snow, or worse. Remember that air is being pushed out of high-pressure systems as it hits the surface and spreads out, while lows tend to suck in air at the surface and pile it up into clouds and storms.

Isobars and Wind Speed

Because lows turn counterclockwise and highs clockwise in the Northern Hemisphere, you can look at an isobar map and tell which way the wind is blowing. Wind blows parallel to isobars above the surface, and the closer together the lines are, the faster the wind speed. In a hurricane, isobars are so tightly packed they almost merge together.

However, down at ground level, the friction caused by air blowing over objects such as mountains, trees, dogs, and people slows down the wind and partially cancels out the Coriolis effect, allowing air to cross isobars as it flows toward low-pressure areas. The section of atmosphere below around 3,300 feet is called the friction layer for that reason.

The isobar maps you see on TV and in the newspaper are called constant height charts because they show equal areas of air pressure at a single height, such as sea level. Another type of map that meteorologists often use is called a constant pressure chart, because it connects areas with the same air pressure whether they're found at the surface or higher in the atmosphere. On a constant pressure chart, meteorologists pick a pressure and show you at which altitude that pressure can be found in different locations.

If you were able to ride along a line on a constant pressure chart, you'd rise and fall as you curved around a low or a high, because air pressure varies by height depending on air temperature and other factors. You can think of isobars on a constant height chart as being narrow speedways around lows or highs, whereas the contour lines on a constant pressure chart are more like roller coasters.

What's Up

While surface maps tell us what the weather is like outside our windows, upper-air maps can tell forecasters what kind of weather we may experience in the near future. With nothing to slow them down, winds aloft almost always blow faster than air that flows along at ground level. Winds in the upper atmosphere generally blow from west to east, creating a zonal flow where the wind follows the lines of latitude that wrap around the earth horizontally. In a zonal flow, storm systems follow the course of least resistance, making a beeline across the country as fast as the wind will carry them. Because temperatures don't differ much within a zonal flow, they don't usually bring severe weather.

So what happens when something comes along to disturb the air's nice straight course; something like a large mass of cold air moving down from Canada, or a big sticky bubble of hot air floating northward from the Gulf of Mexico? Then we have a meridional flow, so-called because those systems move roughly north or south along meridians, the lines that mark off longitude. A meridional flow indicates that air masses from the north and south are mixing, and that can mean stormy weather as areas of differing temperatures battle it out for air superiority.

THE JET STREAM

High-Flying Currents

The jet stream is a river in Earth's atmosphere. It's not even close to being a stream—it's more like an Amazon of flowing air. The jet stream, found anywhere from 6 to 9 miles up in the atmosphere, separates, transports, and steers the giant air masses created by meridional flows as it snakes its way across the country and around the world. The jet stream's speed ranges from around 75 to 200 miles per hour, but it can reach even higher speeds in jet streaks, which are faster-moving areas embedded in the main stream.

Swedish-born meteorologist and Weather Bureau employee Carl-Gustaf Arvid Rossby first proposed the jet stream's existence in 1939. Rossby also discovered that eddies can form in the jet stream, becoming stronger and more powerful until they break up into cells that can be long lasting. His namesake, Rossby waves, which describe the meandering circulations of the jet stream, have since been discovered in the oceans and even on Mars.

Jet Stream Shifts

Jet streams can shift suddenly, bringing abrupt changes in weather with them. When the polar jet plunges deep into the US South, it can cause widespread crop damage. Recently scientists have become concerned about the crossing of the equator by the northern jet stream, something, they say, that could bring "unprecedented change" to the world's weather.

Where the jet stream takes a dive south, a trough is formed; where it moves northward, it forms a ridge. Although local TV forecasters refer to "the" jet stream, there are actually two constantly moving rivers of air in each hemisphere, the polar and subtropical jets. The polar jet, usually found around 60 degrees latitude, is the one most relevant to the United States, marking the boundary between warmer air at lower latitudes and colder Canadian air to the north.

When a big bubble of frigid high-pressure air surges southward into the United States, the boundary between cold and warm air becomes a battleground, causing severe weather in the form of mid-latitude cyclones to break out all along its length. This boundary, marking the leading edge of a cold air mass, is a cold front. Conversely, warm fronts occur when large masses of warm, moist air ride up over the top of cooler air, often causing long periods of rain.

The subtropical jet stream hangs around at 30 degrees latitude, and during the summer it is barely detectable. Though the subtropical jet is much weaker than its polar cousin, at times it can advance northward over the continent and bring moist, unstable air to the upper levels of the atmosphere. In winter the polar and subtropical jet streams can even merge into one, and the resulting super-jet creates extremely strong storms.

Rocky Mountain High

The Rocky Mountains have a major effect on the country's weather, acting as a huge dam between eastern and western air masses. One computer modeling study showed that MCCs (mesoscale convective complexes)—large, circular, long-lived clusters of showers and thunderstorms—develop when rain-cooled air pours down the mountains into a warmer moist air mass on the Great Plains, forcing it to rise and spawn a giant thunderstorm complex.

Jet streams have a huge effect on our daily weather. Once meteorologists were aware of their existence and learned how to predict their movements, they could look upstream and use what they saw to determine with much more accuracy what the weather would be like in the future. Pilots have also learned to take advantage of the jet stream, riding its currents on eastbound routes and avoiding it when flying west.

Meteorogically, jet streams have a much more important purpose: they act as conveyer belts, carrying warm air into the upper latitudes and cool air southward. This heat transfer process is just one way Earth maintains a measure of balance in its atmosphere.

WHAT'S A FRONT?

A Force for Change

Frontal systems are the catalysts of the atmosphere, always bringing a change in the weather as one air mass does its best to shove another one out of the way. Because fronts mark the boundaries of air masses with differing temperatures, humidity levels, and densities, you can usually find clouds and precipitation at these interfaces, unless the air masses are fairly similar in nature.

WARM FRONTS AND COLD FRONTS

As mentioned earlier, warm fronts mark the leading edge of an advancing mass of warmer air where it encounters an area that's colder. The warm air rises over the top of the cold air and begins to cool, and when it reaches the condensation point, clouds and rain form, often far in advance of the actual front. The first sign that a warm front is approaching is often the appearance of cirrus clouds. Those are followed by lower clouds like altostratus and finally a thick layer of stratus or nimbostratus clouds, which can generate a lot of rain and fairly strong winds.

If you could cut a warm front down the middle and view the cross section from the side, you'd notice that it looks like a giant wedge in the sky, with the thinner portion riding over the cooler air. Cirrus clouds are found at the thin end, with the actual front and its clouds and rain at the other. Because of its gentle slope, warm fronts create a gradual change in the weather that can stick around for a day or more, and its rains tend to be less strong but longer lasting than those of a cold front. On a weather map, a warm front is marked by a line with a series of rounded bumps that face in the direction the front is moving, and are red on color charts.

Pushy Weather

In contrast, a cold front, usually associated with low-pressure systems, can move in like a linebacker, bullying the warmer air out of its way. Unlike the gentler warm fronts, cold fronts often bring violent disturbances as they tunnel underneath the warmer air, forcing it rapidly upward and causing a sudden and intense instability in the atmosphere. If the temperature difference between the two air masses is considerable, clouds form rapidly along the front, often growing into towering cumulonimbus in very short order. These clouds form a very well-defined line as they rampage across the countryside, bringing torrential rain, hail, and general unpleasantness to all in their path.

Wind Chill

The wind chill factor is a number that tells you how cold it feels at a particular temperature and humidity level. The method of computing wind chill was recently changed to more accurately reflect real conditions, using wind speeds at 5 feet in height rather than at 33 feet. Now, the wind chill factor also takes into account the danger of frostbite.

After the cold front passes, the temperature can suddenly drop as much as 40°F in just a few hours, and the humidity usually lessens as well. A cross section of a cold front would show a curved bubble of cold air pushing relentlessly underneath a warmer layer. Cold fronts usually move toward the east or south, but occasionally one will make its way westward near the northeast coast, driven by a high-pressure area over Canada. Because it's arriving from the "wrong" direction, these oddball fronts are called back-door cold fronts. On a weather map, cold fronts are depicted as lines with sharp triangles pointing in their direction of motion, and are blue if the map is in color.

Not All Fronts Are Equal

Some cold fronts are worse than others. In the spring and fall there may not be much difference in temperature between the air on either side of a cold front. But on January 23, 1916, in Browning, Montana, the temperature plunged from 44°F to –56°F in less than twenty-four hours after a frontal passage—a world record for the fastest, deepest temperature drop.

Sometimes a cold front catches up to a warm front, creating a hybrid called an occluded front. There are two types of occluded fronts: warm and cold. A cold occlusion occurs when the air behind the occluded front is colder than the air ahead of it. The cold occlusion acts like a cold front, as the cold air behind the front pushes underneath the cool air ahead of it. A warm occlusion occurs when the air behind the occluded front is warmer than the air ahead of it. The warm occlusion acts like a warm front, since the cool air behind the front, which is lighter than the cold air ahead, passes over the top of the cold air. On a map, an occluded front is shown as a line that contains the symbols for both warm and cold fronts, again pointing in the direction of motion. On a color map, an occluded front is purple.

Faltering Fronts

What if a front loses its way and grinds to a halt, like a befuddled driver forced to stop and consult a road map? That's a stationary front, a line that marks the spot where two air masses have fought each other to a draw. That doesn't mean a lack of weather, however. Clouds and rain can still be active on the northern side of the front, and because it's not moving, bad weather can persist for days, causing flooding and general consternation. Stationary fronts often dissipate over time, but if one starts moving again, it turns back into whichever front is more active. Weather maps show stationary fronts as alternating segments of cold and warm fronts, with the half-round warm-front symbols pointing toward the warm air and the cold-front spikes aiming toward the cold side of the front. Stationary fronts alternate red and blue on a color map.

Fronts stall out because the upper-level winds that have been pushing them along change direction. If wind that has been blowing behind the front suddenly starts flowing along it instead, the front loses momentum and finally stops.

MAKING WAVES

Frontal lows are also known as wave cyclones, because the intersection between the warm front and the cold front begins to resemble a wave on a weather map as the cyclone develops. The cold front moves southward as the warm front pushes northward, wrapping around the central low-pressure system. As warm, moist air is drawn around the eastern side of the center and cold, dry air is drawn toward the west, the wave cyclone gains intensity, fueled by heat generated by condensation in the rapidly rising air.

CREATING AN AIR MASS

Air in Motion

Fronts are just the leading edges of much larger air masses, which can cover thousands of square miles. In an air mass, temperatures and moisture levels are similar across the entire length, breadth, and depth of this huge parcel of atmosphere. Because air masses move, creating fronts at their forward edges, they bring the weather conditions from their point of origin to other regions. So, if a large bubble of cold air slides across the Canadian border into the United States and runs into warmer air, it simply shoves the warm air aside, and so places like Ohio or Indiana will experience the same weather Ontario was experiencing twenty-four hours earlier.

AIR MASSES

Air masses like to form in source regions that feature large areas of high pressure, and meteorologists categorize them by the region where they were created. An air mass formed in a tropical area earns the designation "T," while a polar air mass gets tagged with a capital "P." Those forming over land get a lowercase "c" (for continental), while air masses originating over water get an "m" (for maritime). There are also arctic (A) and equatorial (E) air masses.

Mixing and Matching Air Masses

Those designations can be mixed and matched to nail down an air mass's nature, and there are other tags that can be used when more detail is needed. If an air mass is moving over a warmer surface, the letter "k" is used. If the underlying surface is colder, a "w" is added to the designation. This naming system covers any kind of air mass that might form in any environment, anywhere in the world. When a meteorologist sees the letter combination "mPk," he knows it refers to a polar air mass that originated over water and is currently moving over a warmer surface.

Maritime Tropical (mT) air masses, not surprisingly, contain a great deal of moisture. In the winter they can move northward from the Gulf of Mexico, bringing mild weather to the United States's mid-section. In the summer they cause thunderstorms to form, although they usually die out quickly.

Maritime Polar (mP) air also contains a lot of moisture, and mainly affects the Pacific coast of the United States. As they encounter the coast and the mountains farther inland, these systems give up much of their water as rain and snow. Because of the moderating effect caused by moving over water, mP masses aren't nearly as cold as cP air.

Jetting in from the Continent

Continental Polar (cP) and Continental Arctic (cA) air masses bring loads of cold, dry air with them, and they are responsible for the worst winter weather over the United States. Because they originate over Alaska and Canada, there is little moisture in them, and when the jet stream carries them deep into the heartland, long-standing low-temperature records can be broken.

Continental Tropical (cT) air masses, which form in Mexico and the American Southwest, bring hot, dry weather. Driven by a stable high-pressure system, cT air can move into an area like the Midwest and stay for a prolonged visit, causing severe droughts.

All of these air masses occur on a large scale and each is easily identifiable on a weather map of the continental United States. But other wind patterns occur on a much smaller scale. Swirls and eddies of all kinds constantly whirl around us, embedded in the larger air masses that regularly cruise by.

EDDIES, TURBULENCE, AND BREEZES

Eddies that occur on a very small scale affect a limited area such as a single block or a backyard. Many of these eddies are caused by wind running into solid objects such as trees, buildings, cars, and mailboxes that break a straight breeze into a swirling pattern called mechanical turbulence. These swirls become visible when they pick up light objects on the ground, like that big pile of leaves you just finished raking up. Local wind features like these are called microscale winds, the smallest scale of motion measured by meteorologists.

It's strange, but low, low down—within about 0.01 millimeter off the ground—there's almost never any wind at all, no matter how fast the breeze is blowing above. To get picked up and moved, a particle has to be taller than the 0.01 millimeter limit. As these larger particles are picked up and blown around, they can knock other bits into the air, creating dust devils and even dust storms.

All these small disturbances tend to slow down the layers of air above them too. With no obstacles to cause any friction, the air from treetop level up to around 3,300 feet is often moving much faster, sometimes twice as fast, as at the surface. The area where turbulence interacts with smooth-flowing air is called the boundary layer, or friction layer.

When the Sun heats the ground and those bubbles of warm air begin to rise, thermal turbulence adds to the general atmospheric mixing caused by mechanical turbulence, and the lower atmosphere can get fairly unstable. As the afternoon progresses, these turbulent eddies grow stronger, producing strong, gusty winds down at the surface.

Deadly Eddies

When these eddie swirls form high in the atmosphere, they give airline pilots and their passengers yet another thing to worry about. Where winds suddenly change speed and direction, they produce a dangerous condition called wind shear, which can cause an aircraft to quickly gain or lose a great deal of altitude without warning. At lower altitudes, that can be deadly. Below a height of around 2,000 feet, with a commercial airliner on final approach, the pilot is forced to reduce speed and has very little time to react to violent changes in wind speed or direction.

LIDAR

Wind shear can now be detected with a technology called LIDAR (Light Detection and Ranging), which uses a laser instead of radar's microwave beam. The laser reflects off the dust and other small particles in the atmosphere, and their images appear on a monitor, providing instant data on wind speed and direction.

On August 2, 1985, a Delta L-1011 was on final approach to Dallas/Fort Worth International Airport when it was hit by a violent downdraft caused by wind shear. Unable to gain altitude, the pilot lost control of the plane, which collided with several objects on the ground before crashing into a water tank near the runway. One hundred thirty-three people were killed and thirty-one injured in the crash, which brought a public outcry for more sophisticated methods of detecting wind shear. After the crash, the Federal Aviation Administration undertook a large-scale project to modernize equipment at major airports, including wind shear detectors and improved Doppler radar.

In the Dallas incident, controllers might have been alerted to the turbulence by the presence of a small thunderstorm nearby if more had been known about wind shear at the time. But another type of wind shear, clear-air turbulence, often gives no visible clue to its existence until the plane is in its grip. On December 28, 1997, United Airlines Flight 826 from Tokyo to Honolulu ran into a pocket of clear-air turbulence 5 miles up. The plane started to shake, and then unexpectedly dropped 100 feet. Oxygen masks deployed, and anyone not wearing their seat belts flew up and crashed against the ceiling of the cabin. The plane made it back to Japan for an emergency landing, but eighty-three people were injured and one passenger was killed in the incident.

To prevent this kind of accident, NASA (National Aeronautics and Space Administration) has begun a program called SCATCAT (Severe Clear-Air Turbulence Colliding with Air Traffic) that will try to find new ways of detecting turbulence before it can cause a disaster.

Wind and Water

While microscale winds occur in a relatively small area, mesoscale systems can encompass from fifty to several hundred square miles. If you've ever been to the beach in the afternoon, you've experienced one of the more common examples of a mesoscale system known as the sea breeze, which you'll find anywhere there's a boundary between sea and land. Because the land heats up more quickly than the ocean, during the day the air over land areas rises and expands from the Sun's heat, creating a weak thermal low-pressure system. The cooler air over the water begins to flow into this low, refreshing beachgoers with a cooling breeze.

At night it's the other way around: the land cools off more rapidly than the water, producing a weak high-pressure system. Since air flows from highs toward lows, the sea breeze turns into a land breeze that flows back toward the ocean.

A WIND BY ANY OTHER NAME

Mesoscale winds are known by many names according to their type, location, and season. For instance, the warm, dry wind that flows down the eastern slopes of the Rocky Mountains is called a Chinook. Strong westerly winds blow over the Rockies and fall down the eastern slopes, and the air gets compressed and heated as it descends. Because the wind loses most of its moisture on the western, windward side of the mountains, it brings dry, warmer air to the eastern valleys.

A monsoon is a wind that blows one way in the summer and the other way in winter, such as the winds found in the Indian Ocean. Like sea breezes, monsoon winds are a result of the land's ability to warm more rapidly than the sea. During the summertime the Asian continent is heated until it's much warmer than the ocean to its south. The resulting pressure gradient causes air to flow from the Indian Ocean up into India, where it can cause heavy rain and severe flooding. In the winter, arctic air and radiational cooling over land reverse the flow, and cold, dry air rushes south toward the sea.

Residents of the Los Angeles Basin are familiar with the hot, dry Santa Ana winds, which flow down from the high desert. When a high pressure area forms in the Great Basin east of the Sierra Nevada mountain range, it forces air downslope, causing it to compress and heat up at the rate of about 5°F for every 1,000 feet it falls. Because Santa Ana winds bring extremely dry air, they also bring a higher likelihood of wildfires in the affected areas.

The Sahara desert is home to the sirocco, another hot, dry wind caused when a low-pressure system forms in the Mediterranean south of Spain and France. A sirocco can blow dust from northern Africa all the way to Europe.

Coastal residents from Maine to the Philippines have learned to live with the storms that are part of life at the sea's edge, but the ocean's effects don't stop at the shoreline. In fact the earth's seas influence the global climate more than any other factor.

OCEANS AND WEATHER

A Symbiotic Relationship

"In all my experience, I have never been in any accident . . . or any sort worth speaking about."

—E.J. Smith, captain, RMS *Titanic*

Not only are the oceans capable of sinking large ocean liners, but they also team up with the atmosphere to create long-standing climate conditions all over the globe. This power makes them the biggest influence of all on the earth's weather and climate.

RIVERS IN THE SEA

Knowing that giant rivers of air meander through the atmosphere, it probably wouldn't surprise you to find that the oceans have their own streams and eddies as well. Prevailing winds get surface waters moving along with them, and the effect transfers down through the ocean layers, creating currents that span entire seas. Even deeper currents are caused by the water's density. The sea is denser at greater depths because cold water is heavier than warmer water; the molecules in frigid water have been squeezed closer together. Seawater also contains salt, which makes it heavier than fresh water.

In the 1500s, Juan Ponce de León, who had arrived in the New World on Columbus's second voyage, discovered that his ship was unable to make headway while sailing south from Saint Augustine in what is now Florida, even though the wind was behind him. Unaware of it at the time the explorer was trying to sail against the Gulf Stream, part of a vast river of water that circles the entire Atlantic Ocean. Later, conquistadors learned to take advantage of this current by riding it to a point where prevailing winds could carry them back to Spain.

GENTLY DOWN THE STREAM

The Gulf Stream originates, fittingly enough, with the strong currents flowing into the Gulf of Mexico from the Caribbean, then moves eastward through the Straits of Florida between Florida and Cuba, where it's called the Florida Current. It then joins the Antilles Current and flows north along the southeastern coast of the United States.

When the Gulf Stream encounters North Carolina's east coast at Cape Hatteras, it begins to turn eastward, eventually running into the Labrador Current off Newfoundland, where it creates heavy layers of fog over the ocean. In this area, the Gulf Stream has now lost much of its warmth and becomes the North Atlantic Current, which crosses the Atlantic on prevailing southwest winds and begins to turn south near the coast of Europe. There, it joins with the Canary Current to form the North Equatorial Current. Now the cycle begins again as the North Equatorial Current heads west toward the United States again.

In the Gulf of Mexico, the Gulf Stream is about 50 miles wide and surges along at about 4 miles per hour, making it one of the strongest currents known. But in the North Atlantic, it slows to only 1 mile per hour and splits into several smaller currents that total several hundred miles in width. At this point, the current moves 500 times more water per second than the Amazon River. The frigid North Atlantic causes the moving water to sink, creating a deep current that keeps the Gulf Stream moving in its constant circular journey.

Current Information

The Gulf Stream is only one giant whorl of water, although it's the best known in the United States. There are similar circular currents in the Western Pacific and other oceans. These currents, like the flowing air masses above them, serve to transport heat northward. The earth's oceans absorb about half of all the solar radiation streaming through the atmosphere, creating a huge source of potential energy. If all this energy wasn't balanced by the oceans' heat transfer process, there would eventually be a huge temperature difference between southern and northern latitudes, causing dire and far-reaching consequences for the global climate.

The Sargasso Sea

In the middle of the North Atlantic is a gyre. This vast ocean-within-an-ocean is called the Sargasso Sea. Caught between coastal Atlantic currents, its sluggish waters collect seaweed, driftwood, and other floating debris that are home to a multitude of tiny sea creatures.

The scientific term for giant circling currents is "gyre." Five gyres dominate the planet's oceans, one each in the North Pacific, South Pacific, North Atlantic, South Atlantic, and Indian Ocean. Because of the Coriolis effect (for details, see the section titled High Pressure and Low Pressure), the water circling around each gyre tends to deflect to the right. This has the effect of moving the water inward, creating a dome of water at the center of each one. There may be a difference of only a few feet between the height of the dome and the gyre's edge, but that's enough to make the surface water eventually flow back "downhill," where it joins and reinforces the stream's current.

Wandering Flows

Even though the Gulf Stream and other ocean currents are permanent features, you won't always find them in exactly the same place. Not only do they tend to meander a bit, but occasionally an eddy will break away and go spinning off by itself, carrying the characteristics of the region where it formed to other parts of the ocean, just as an air mass does in the atmosphere. Scientists can sample water from one of these large whirlpools and learn where it originated. In fact in one case, small surface eddies from 500 miles off Cape Hatteras were found to have begun in the far eastern Atlantic near Gibraltar, more than 2,500 miles away!

When we think of currents we think horizontally, but there are vertical currents in the ocean, too, known as upwellings. When surface waters are moving away from each other, or diverging, more water from underneath comes up to replace them, usually bringing colder, nutrient-rich water to the surface. Fish go where the food is, so upwelling can make a summertime fishing expedition a more rewarding experience while also cooling nearby shores. Upwelling usually occurs near a coastline, where winds blow surface water away from the shore. When the waters are blown back toward the coast, downwelling can occur as surface water gets compressed against the shore and sinks toward the bottom.

EL NIÑO

A Warmer Ocean

The oceans have always been known as major influences on the earth's climate, but the extent of the seas' effects wasn't known until the last few years. In the 1800s, fishermen along the coasts of Ecuador and Peru noted that sometimes the ocean would become much warmer offshore around Christmastime, so they named this thermal change El Niño, which in Spanish means "the Christ child."

Normally, cold water upwelling from the depths along the coasts makes for good fishing, since it contains nutrients that attract large colonies of anchovies and other types of fish. But during an El Niño event, fish became scarce due to the warmer water, so the fishermen would take time off to maintain their boats, repair their nets, and spend some quality time at home. Most often their break would last from a few weeks to a month, but at other times these warm periods would last much longer than usual, bringing not only warmer sea temperatures but heavy rains as well, and the South American fishing economy suffered as a result.

Winds between 0 degrees (the equator) and 30 degrees latitude generally blow from west to east and are called the Tropical Easterlies, or "trade" winds, since early sailors depended on them to propel their ships. Normally, these prevailing winds blow warm surface water from areas of higher pressure in the eastern Pacific all the way across the ocean, where it piles up in low-pressure areas near western Pacific landmasses such as Indonesia. The surface waters literally do pile up, actually raising the sea level in those areas.

As you've learned, water follows wind, so some of the cooler water from the coast of South America is pulled westward; and as it's dragged along, it warms up from the Sun's energy. The result is a huge area of warmer water in the western Pacific (containing thirty or forty times more water than all the Great Lakes combined), and cooler water in the eastern regions.

Every few years, the trade winds weaken, and atmospheric pressure starts to rise in the western Pacific while it drops in the eastern Pacific. The trade winds reverse direction, and a giant dome of warm water about 5 feet high, El Niño, begins moving back across the ocean toward South America, where water levels begin to rise. In the western Pacific the levels drop and can actually dip below sea level as the ocean sloshes back toward the east. If you've ever tried to carry a pan full of water very far, you're familiar with the sloshing effect, up one side of the pan and then the other. All the warm water heading east can bring torrential rains and flooding in Peru. Meanwhile on the other side of the ocean, Australia and Indonesia can be experiencing droughts. El Niño rides up over colder water near the South American coast, forcing it downward and choking off the supply of fish that many depend upon for their livelihoods.

EL NIÑO–SOUTHERN OSCILLATION

When water is sloshing around in a pan it's oscillating, and when the Pacific sloshes back and forth it's called the El Niño–Southern Oscillation, or ENSO. El Niños happen about every two to seven years, on average, and every one is different in both its strength and its effects on the global economy.

With the kind of energy El Niño has, it's not hard to see how these events can cause radical changes in climate across the entire globe. Because the ENSO effect has only been recognized for a relatively brief amount of time, scientists are still building databases that will enable them to try and predict the next one. The Pacific experienced one of the strongest El Niños ever in 1982, and by the time it had faded the following year, nearly 2,000 lives had been lost, hundreds of thousands of people were left homeless, and damage estimates were in the $13 billion range.

The Longest-Lasting El Niño

The El Niño that began in 1991 lasted until 1995, which is about three to four times longer than average. It also brought the worst drought in southern Africa of the twentieth century, affecting nearly 100 million people.

With friends like El Niño, the earth doesn't need enemies. Despite all the damage caused by El Niño–generated weather events, these occurrences do have a beneficial side. Hurricanes often form near the western coast of Africa in the summer and travel westward across the Atlantic on the prevailing winds. But in an El Niño year, winds blowing from the west shear off the tops of developing tropical systems, nipping them in the bud before they can get cranked up. Scientists have also found that the increased plant growth caused by heavier-than-average rainfall may trigger a drop in carbon dioxide, a so-called greenhouse gas often implicated in the increase of global warming.

EL NIÑO'S FLIP SIDE

When an El Niño finally loosens its grip on the Pacific, conditions sometimes shift into reverse and a La Niña (the girl child) event begins. Conditions during a La Niña are the opposite of an El Niño: areas that were flooded dry out, and instead of fewer hurricanes, stronger and more frequent storms ply the south Atlantic and the Caribbean.

During a La Niña, also called El Viejo (old man) or the anti-El Niño, high pressure near Tahiti and low pressure over Australia strengthen the trade winds, causing surface waters near Peru to blow out to sea. As they depart, cold water from deep in the ocean rises to take their place, and the Pacific's surface temperature begins to drop.

La Niñas don't form quite as often—only about every two to ten years—but their effects on the United States can be just as important as El Niños'. Because the jet stream is diverted into a more serpentine flow during a La Niña year, winter temperatures are warmer than normal in the Southeast and cooler and wetter than normal in the Northwest. La Niña can cause droughts in the American Southwest while bringing much colder weather to the upper Midwestern states. Although it doesn't usually cause as many problems as El Niño, La Niña's effects can last much longer.

ENSOs and Climate Modeling

No two ENSOs are exactly alike, so statistics tell you only the likelihood of a certain condition, not what causes it. That's where climate modeling—creating a virtual world using simulated weather conditions—comes into play. Data from actual weather analysis is fed in, and analysts can see how close the results are to actual observations.

As the implications of the ENSO have become more obvious, research into the phenomenon and attempts to predict it have gone into overdrive. The 1997 event was the first one ever to be successfully predicted, when the National Oceanic and Atmospheric Administration (NOAA) announced in April of that year the possibility that a strong El Niño would soon form. We now know it to be the strongest ENSO event in recorded history.

Meteorologists use several tools to predict future atmospheric conditions, including El Niños and La Niñas. One is statistical analysis, where scientists examine past weather records to uncover trends that might give them clues to future conditions. Analysts can compile statistics and compare conditions in, say, the eastern Pacific during El Niño years, combine them with statistics on conditions in the western Pacific, and use the results to determine what usually happens in those areas during a warm ENSO event.

PREDICTING ENSO PREDICAMENTS

In 1997, for the very first time, meteorologists used climate modeling to forecast El Niño, and came up with a prediction that was more accurate than one obtained by statistical analysis. This is an extremely important development for industries, such as agriculture, that depend on the weather. One reason the 1982–1983 El Niño was so devastating to crops is that it wasn't predicted or even recognized until it was well under way.

After that experience, the Peruvian government undertook a program to predict future ENSO events, realizing their country would be ground zero for every climatic fluctuation. After the system was developed, a forecast for the upcoming growing season was released to the minister of agriculture, indicating that it would be a good year with near-normal rainfall. Sure enough, the forecast was correct, and the government began releasing its predictions each year in November, giving farmers a heads-up on what to plant. If an El Niño is forecast, they can plant water-loving crops like rice, and if La Niña is coming, something more drought-tolerant like cotton can be substituted.

In the United States, the forecasting picture is much rosier than it was in the 1980s. Recognizing that the ENSO knows no boundaries, the United States and France teamed up to launch TOPEX/Poseidon, a satellite system that uses a sophisticated radar altimeter to measure sea levels with an accuracy of within 4 inches. The satellite emits a radar beam that bounces off the ocean surface and returns; by measuring how long it takes for the beam to come back, the distance to the surface and hence the sea level can be determined. Its follow-up program, a satellite called Jason-1, is hoped to be accurate to within less than 1 inch. As sea levels rise in some places and fall in others when an ENSO event is beginning, much earlier warnings will be available to farmers, governments, and the general public, and loss of life and property can be minimized.

SOLAR WIND

Weather and the Sun

Ancient civilizations knew how important the Sun's light was for growing crops, although they weren't aware that the Sun is just an ordinary star like the ones they saw twinkling in the sky. Actually, they didn't know what stars were either, but that's a story for another book.

What they certainly didn't know is that the Sun is a gigantic thermonuclear furnace that continually fuses hydrogen into helium deep in its core and releases huge amounts of energy in both visible and invisible wavelengths. The fusion process is very difficult to achieve here on Earth because great pressure and temperature are required, but it's a snap for Old Sol since temperatures at the inner 25 percent of its core (where most of the fusion reactions occur) average around 27,000,000°F. In the heart of the Sun it's not the humidity; it's the heat.

Avoid Looking

Remember, the Sun is really only visible if you're wearing suitable eye protection or are viewing it through an approved solar filter. Never, ever look at the Sun, even for a moment, without proper eye protection.

Just as with Earth's atmosphere, scientists divide the Sun's layers into zones. Energy generated in the Sun's core gradually works its way toward the surface through convection, and on reaching the photosphere, which is the outer luminous layer that we can see from Earth, becomes visible as light.

LAYERS OF LIGHT

The photosphere is the layer that contains sunspots, huge areas of cooler gases that were first discovered by Galileo back in 1610. In this case "cooler" is a relative term—sunspots are only about 3,000°F less than the photosphere's average temperature of 10,000 to 12,000°F, so you'd still need a sunscreen with a rating of at least SPF one *million* to get anywhere near one. Sunspots are thought to be caused by magnetic fields deep in the Sun that break the surface, creating dark blotches that are often a sign of increased activity deep in the Sun's interior. Sunspots range in size from roughly Earth-sized to more than twenty times the diameter of our planet.

The next layer out is the chromosphere, which is virtually invisible from Earth except during a total solar eclipse, when it can be seen as a narrow red or pink band around the Sun. The chromosphere's temperature is around 14,400°F at the bottom and 36,000°F at the top, so it actually gets hotter as you move away from the Sun. Solar flares originate in the chromosphere, releasing as much energy as a million hydrogen bombs going off at the same time.

The next layer of the Sun's atmosphere is the corona, which is thousands of times fainter than the photosphere and is invisible from Earth except, again, during a total solar eclipse. At that time the corona appears as an elongated, ragged halo around the Sun, with thin white filaments stretching out millions of miles into space like celestial cirrus clouds.

Consistent with the chromosphere, the corona continues to get hotter as distance from the core increases. The temperature of the corona varies from 2,000,000°F to nearly 4,000,000°F. How does the corona get so hot with a cooler layer below it? Astrophysicists think that huge magnetic bands in the photosphere generate massive amounts of electricity and carry it up into the corona. There are tens of thousands of these magnetic loops scattered around the surface of the Sun, and any one of them could satisfy the US's electrical needs for a hundred years if it could somehow be harnessed.

THE WIND FROM THE SUN

The corona isn't static; it continually blasts charged particles out into space, creating the heliosphere, an area of the Sun's influence that actually extends out beyond the orbit of Pluto. These particles, collectively called the solar wind, can cause big problems for the earth when the Sun gets active. The Sun's average distance from Earth is some 93,000,000 miles, but even small changes in its output can have major consequences here, as happens when huge bubbles of plasma erupt in the Sun's outer layers. Such events blow billions of tons of particles from the Sun's atmosphere in a blast called a coronal mass ejection (CME).

Early Warnings

If a CME is directed toward Earth, it smashes into our atmosphere at a million miles an hour, sometimes damaging satellites and causing power and communications disruptions. That's why NOAA and the US Air Force now jointly operate the Space Weather Prediction Center (SWPC), which provides warnings of impending solar explosions.

It's a good thing Earth has a magnetosphere, which deflects most of the particles back into space. But some of the energy from a solar storm can still leak into the atmosphere near the poles where the magnetosphere is weaker, creating the aurora borealis, or northern lights. When appearing over the Southern Hemisphere, the lights are called the aurora australis.

Since the time of Copernicus in the sixteenth century, most people have understood that Earth revolves around the Sun. But the origin of the seasons has often been misunderstood, and even today there are misconceptions about it. When you put your hand close to a stove it gets hot, and when you move it away, it cools. So it would seem that when Earth is closer to the Sun it would be summertime, and when it is farther away, you'd have winter. Earth does indeed get closer and then farther from the Sun during the year because its orbit is slightly elliptical, or oval, but that fact has very little effect on the seasons.

In fact, Earth is closest to the Sun in January, when it's winter in the Northern Hemisphere. In addition, if the seasons were caused by Earth's proximity to the Sun, every country on the planet would experience winter and summer at the same time. But when it's summer in the Southern Hemisphere, it's winter in the Northern. What gives? It all has to do with Earth's tilt and its orbit around the Sun.

ORBITS AND OCEANS

How Much Solar Radiation?

The reason you get to experience winter, spring, summer, and fall is because the amount of sunlight hitting the earth's surface varies throughout the year, and that's a result of the planet's tilt. Earth rotates around an imaginary axle—its axis—that runs from the North Pole to the South. If you picture Earth's orbit as a flat plane around the Sun, that axis is tilted 23.5 degrees away from that plane, called the plane of the ecliptic. In other words, Earth is actually leaning to the side. This means that as Earth orbits the sun, sometimes the Northern Hemisphere is tilted toward the Sun and gets more sunlight, and sometimes the Southern Hemisphere is tilted toward the Sun and gets more sunlight.

The Martian Winter

If there were Martians, they'd experience even more seasonal variations than Earthlings. Mars's orbit is more eccentric than any other planet (except Mercury), and it's tilted on its axis at a slightly more acute angle than Earth. During a Martian winter, a complex carbon dioxide exchange with its polar ice caps causes the planet's atmospheric pressure to drop about 25 percent lower than in summer.

Solar radiation has the most effect on the earth's surface and atmosphere when it's shining straight down. If you shine a flashlight on the middle of a beach ball, you'll notice it makes a round circle, because all the light is focused on that one point. But shine it closer to the top and the beam spreads out into an oval such that there's less light shining on any one spot. That's what happens as Earth revolves around the Sun. From June to September, when the Northern Hemisphere is tilted toward the Sun, light shines more directly on it (which is why the Sun seems to be almost straight overhead) and heats up the surface, causing a run on air conditioners. In addition, these days are longer, so the Sun has more time to do its job.

From December to March, with the Northern Hemisphere tilted away from the Sun, there's less light reaching any one place to warm it up, and there's a run on space heaters. Days are shorter, so by the time the Sun has begun to warm up the atmosphere, it's already descending toward the horizon. Also, with sunlight striking the planet at a lower angle, its rays have to penetrate through a lot more atmosphere to get to the surface, and there's a greater chance that some of that light will get scattered by dust particles, reflected by clouds, or absorbed by gases. Another factor that keeps the surface of Earth from heating up in the winter is the presence of ice or snow, which is very reflective and can keep the Sun's energy from ever reaching the ground.

If Earth didn't tilt, the Sun would always shine directly down on the equator and the days and nights would always be the same length: twelve hours. There would be no seasons, and it would be very hot in the equatorial regions. North America would always receive about the same amount of light it gets between September and December, so most of the time it would probably feel like autumn.

ORBITS AND OCEANS

Drawn on a piece of paper, the orbits of Earth and the other planets are made to look like perfect circles, but in truth, none of them are.

Earth's orbit is about 2 percent closer to the Sun in January than it is in July (other planets' orbits are even more out-of-round), but as mentioned earlier, that small difference isn't enough to affect the seasons very much. The atmosphere receives only about 7 percent more energy when closest to the Sun (perihelion) than it does when farthest away (aphelion). What *does* have an effect is the fact that the earth's landmasses aren't evenly distributed; the Northern Hemisphere has more land; the Southern Hemisphere has more water. Land heats more rapidly than water, so in July when the Sun is shining more directly on landmasses, the temperature of the entire globe is higher than it is in December, when the Sun shines down on the oceans to the south.

You can see that effect on a smaller scale when you visit the desert in the summertime. During the night, the temperature might get down to 60°F or so, but when the Sun comes up, it can rise to over 100°F. If you're sailing on the ocean, however, the temperature might be only 75–80°F. Then, when the Sun goes down, the temperature will fall only a few degrees because water is great at absorbing and retaining heat.

DETERMINING THE SEASONS

The Changing Year

We're acutely tuned to the seasons, whether sunbathing and planning beach trips during the height of summer or groaning at the prospect of shoveling our drive during a winter snowstorm. But what causes the seasonal shifts in the weather? And why do the seasons differ depending on where on the globe we live?

Hello Summer

If you could push a button and fast-forward through an entire year, starting on the first day of summer, you could easily see how each season correlates to Earth's position in its orbit. On June 21, known as the summer solstice, the Sun's rays beat directly down on the Northern Hemisphere. Because Earth is tilted at 23.5 degrees, the Sun shines straight above 23.5 degrees latitude, an imaginary line around Earth called the Tropic of Cancer.

The Longest Day but Not the Hottest

Why is the longest day of the year not also the hottest? Thermal inertia—the tendency of temperatures to remain the same—keeps the land and water from getting instantly hot. Only after several weeks of intense Sun beating down on Earth will the hemisphere start to heat up.

If you stand on this line on the first day of summer, the Sun will be directly overhead, seemingly paused for a moment before beginning to sink lower in the sky each day. This is also the longest day of the year in the entire Northern Hemisphere, and from that first day of summer until December 21 (the winter solstice), the days will get progressively shorter. With the Sun at its highest point, and the days at their longest, common sense would tell you that June should be the hottest month of the year. But due to an effect called thermal inertia, the ocean and landmasses take time to heat up. As a result, the hottest weather usually arrives about six weeks after the summer solstice.

Goodbye Summer

By the time the heat kicks in, you're well on your way to the autumnal equinox on September 22—the first day of fall—when the days and nights are the same length. The oceans in the Northern Hemisphere are at their warmest and tropical storms and hurricanes begin to form. The weather has been getting cooler in the Northern Hemisphere, and now the leaves of many trees begin to show their true colors. On the days following the fall equinox, the Sun begins to set at the North Pole, and six long cold months of darkness set in there, while at the South Pole the Sun is rising.

Autumn Colors

The brilliant reds and oranges of fall are actually right there in the leaves all year long, but because the green color of chlorophyll is so dominant, you can't see them until the chlorophyll level decreases. Cooler nights and shorter days reduce the amount of chlorophyll and allow the leaves to begin their yearly show.

Autumn Leaves, Winter Arrives

As the days get shorter and the weather cooler, cold fronts begin to plow southward and some mornings reveal frost on the lawn. As the winter holidays approach, ice and snow can make an appearance, and by the time the first day of winter arrives on December 21, the Sun is shining directly down on the Southern Hemisphere at 23.5 degrees south—the Tropic of Capricorn—and the days are at their shortest in the North.

At the beginning of winter, the Northern Hemisphere is tilted as far back from the Sun as it can get, so the light reaching the ground is dimmer and more diffuse than at any other time of the year. Again the ground and the oceans are slow to give up the heat they've absorbed through the summer and fall, so the coldest weather is still to come.

Welcome to Spring

As heating bills skyrocket and some cities in the North are hit by blizzards and ice storms, everyone gets tired of being indoors and wishes for spring. Then seed and garden catalogs begin to arrive, just making things worse. By March 20, just about everyone north of 35 degrees north of the equator has gone stir-crazy, but just in time, the first day of spring arrives. On that date, called the vernal equinox, the days and nights are once again equal in length, and the Sun is directly above the equator.

As the Sun rises higher in the sky each day, the land is warmed and trees begin to leaf out again, hibernating animals wake up and begin to search for food, and many people put away their treadmills. The days are getting longer, and before you know it, June is here and you're back where you started. Unfortunately, you're also a year older.

SEASONS AND CIRCLES

In this century, Earth's northern axis points toward Polaris, the North Star. It won't always, though, because Earth's axis wobbles very slowly, about a half a degree per century, like a top just before it stops and falls over. This motion, called precession, causes the planet's axis to describe a giant narrow circle in the sky that takes nearly 26,000 years to complete. So, in about 11,000 years, Earth will be closer to the Sun in July and farther away in December, the opposite of today's situation. In 26,000 years things will be back the way they are now.

Further complicating the picture is the fact that Earth's 23.5-degree tilt changes over time too, taking about 41,000 years to run through a full cycle that varies from about 21.5 to 24.5 degrees. When the angle is smaller, there will be less seasonal variation at middle latitudes; with a larger angle, the variations will be amplified. It's thought that this change in tilt angle is one of the main factors that causes the periodic ice ages that sweep across our planet.

Ice Age Calendars

Archaeologists have found man-made lunar calendars that date back thousands of years. They indicate that Ice Age hunters carved notches and bored holes into sticks, mammoth tusks, and reindeer bones to record the days between each phase of the Moon.

Because the weather was tied to survival, most cultures kept records of its changes and erected monuments that acted as giant seasonal clocks. The most famous of these is Stonehenge, north of Salisbury, England. There is still disagreement as to the ancient stone circle's exact purpose, but because the structure is aligned with the winter and summer solstices, many feel it functioned as a predictor of the passage of the seasons for the early residents of Britain.

At Machu Picchu, Peru's City in the Clouds, the ancient Incas set up the Intihuatana ("Hitching Post of the Sun"), a stone that precisely indicated the date of the winter solstice. The ceremony they performed there was designed to halt the Sun in its northern migration through the sky. Machu Picchu's Temple of the Sun features a window exactly aligned with the sunrise on the summer solstice.

THE DATING GAME

The Egyptians were keen students of the Sun and stars, and around 3,000 B.C. they created a calendar very similar to the one used today. Like clockwork, the Nile river would flood each year at about the same time, and Egyptian sky watchers noted that the star Sirius would rise into the sky around that time too. The period between appearances was 365.25 days, so the Egyptians based their calendar on that time period. This calendar was later copied by Julius Caesar.

In the Americas, ancient tribes had their own ways of predicting the seasons. The early residents of Wyoming built a large circle made of stones that seems to point toward the position of the Sun at the summer solstice. The structure, known as the Bighorn Medicine Wheel, lies at an altitude of nearly 10,000 feet in the mountains.

Our ancestors did the best they could to use the Sun, the Moon, and the stars as predictors of coming climatic conditions, and some succeeded amazingly well. Their early research paved the way for the more sophisticated instruments of forecasting to come. But it's a tribute to their resourcefulness and ingenuity that many of their methods of predicting the seasons still work today.

DEVELOPING THERMOMETERS

Taking the Temperature

When Galileo created a device he called a thermoscope in 1593, it was really just an interesting toy. Galileo's device had no markings to indicate degrees; that task would fall to his friends Santorio Santorio and Gianfrancesco Sagredo, who were the first to apply a crude numerical scale to the thermograph, making it the first official air thermometer. At the same time, similar devices were being developed all over Europe, but each inventor worked independently, so there was no universally agreed-upon scale of measurement.

A few decades later, Amsterdam instrument maker Daniel Gabriel Fahrenheit came along with access to more responsive alcohol thermometers. Still, there was no temperature-measuring scale everyone could agree on. After Fahrenheit invented an even more sensitive thermometer, filled with mercury, he decided a universal heat measuring system was needed.

Fahrenheit filled a container with salt and ice water to obtain the lowest temperature he could and called that point 0°F, then he measured the temperature of melting ice without the salt and assigned it the value of 30°F. His own body temperature was marked at 96°F. When he later added the boiling point of water to his scale, at 212°F, he changed the melting point of water to 32°F so that the scale would balance out at an even 180°F between the melting and boiling points of water—the angle of a straight line. On the new scale, body temperature came out to 98.6°F.

HOT COMPETITION

Seems pretty confusing, doesn't it? Maybe that's why Swedish astronomer Anders Celsius suggested a simpler system in 1742. His method divided the difference between water's melting and boiling points into one hundred equal parts. Using the Celsius scale, room temperature is around 25°C, while a hot summer day can reach 30–38°C. Water freezes at 0°C and boils at 100°C. What could be easier?

Since there were now two temperature scales to choose from, there was no need to further complicate matters, right? Sir William Thomson, a Scottish mathematician also known as Lord Kelvin, apparently didn't think so. Kelvin wanted to eliminate the need for negative numbers when measuring temperature, so in 1848 he devised a temperature scale that started at the lowest possible temperature, absolute zero. That works out to -273.18°C, or -459°F. His scale is called (surprise!) the Kelvin, or thermodynamic, scale.

Absolute Zero

The Third Law of Thermodynamics prohibits the temperature from reaching absolute zero, even in space. Although there doesn't seem to be an upper limit on heat, the temperature in deep space never gets below 2.7 K due to background radiation left over from the Big Bang. If it could get to absolute zero, all motion right down to the atomic level would stop.

The science of measuring temperature has come a long way since then. Bimetal thermometers depend on the expansion and contraction rates of two different metals to move a pointer that indicates temperature. Others measure the high and low temperatures over a given time. Radiometric thermometers measure temperature by reading an object's radiation emission spectrum. Liquid-crystal thermometers change color with the temperature, like a 1970s mood ring. These days, the thermometer you're mostly likely to encounter is electronic. Such a thermometer uses a device called a thermistor that measures resistance through an internal element.

THE TOOLS OF METEOROLOGY

Barometers and Other Mysterious Gadgets

Grand Duke Ferdinand II of Tuscany was the first to notice that barometric pressure dropped during storms. And in 1660 the barometer was used to predict the weather for the first time by Otto von Guericke, mayor of Magdeburg, Germany.

In 1844, the first barometer that didn't use a liquid was patented by Lucien Vidie, a French scientist who based his invention on a small vacuum chamber attached to a pointer that would rise and fall as the atmospheric pressure made the chamber expand and contract. He called his barometer an aneroid, from a Greek word meaning "without water." Vidie's invention is still in use today, as are mercury-filled varieties, but the electronics revolution has helped create a much more advanced version of the barometer.

An electronic barometer uses an electrical sensor to measure minute changes in atmospheric pressure, and sends the readings to a digital display. Originally very expensive, these barometers are now available to home users either as a stand-alone instrument or as part of a home weather station to help you predict coming weather conditions. Barometers have changed quite a bit since Pascal's brother-in-law climbed Puy de Dôme with one in 1648!

WHY IT'S A BAD HAIR DAY

Of course, the more instruments you have, the more accurate your forecasts will be. Determining how much moisture the air contains is one of the most important measurements you can make.

The instrument used to measure humidity is called a hygrometer, invented in 1780 by Horace de Saussure, a Swiss meteorologist and geologist. De Saussure based his invention on the fact that hair becomes longer when the air is humid and shorter when it's dry. He attached small levers to human hairs that measured the change in length, correlating to how much water vapor the air held.

Relative Humidity

Relative humidity can actually exceed 100 percent. When the temperature drops below the dew point, air can become supersaturated with moisture, raising the humidity to a higher percentage. But the condition is just temporary: the moisture will condense into fog or dew fairly quickly, and the relative humidity will once again be 100 percent.

The hair hygrometer was rather inaccurate, leading to the invention of the sling psychrometer: two thermometers mounted side by side. One is covered with a wick that is moistened with water, while the other is kept dry, and the unit is spun around for a few minutes. Water evaporating from the wet side will cool the thermometer, lowering the reading below the actual air temperature. The drier the air, the greater the evaporation, and, therefore, the greater the difference between the two temperatures. The difference tells the reader how much water the air can hold versus how much it's currently holding—the relative humidity. The sling psychrometer has largely been replaced by the electronic hygrometer.

The Dew Point

This is probably a good time to address the dew point. You know it's important because weather forecasters mention it often, but it's rarely well explained. Just remember that the warmer the air is, the more water vapor it can hold. When the air can no longer hold any more water, condensation occurs. When this change happens up in the clouds, it forms rain; on the ground it makes dew. So the dew point is the temperature at which the vapor in the air will begin to condense. For instance, if the current temperature is 80°F and a forecaster says the dew point is 70, you know it has to get ten degrees cooler before dew can form.

CATCHING THE WIND

The instrument that tells you how fast the wind is blowing is an anemometer. Leonardo da Vinci usually gets credit for inventing the first one, which he designed around 1500. But the first working model was put together by Robert Hooke in 1667. Hooke's version used a hanging plate of metal hinged at the top; when the wind blew, the plate would swing out at an angle and the wind speed could be read off a scale attached to the side of the instrument. Today's anemometers use three or more cups mounted on a vertical shaft. The speed of the cups' rotation translates directly to wind speed; the data can then be transmitted to an electronic base station that displays the information.

The oldest weather instrument is no doubt the wind vane, which reveals which way the wind is blowing. The earliest known wind vane stood atop the Tower of the Winds in Athens, Greece, which was built around 48 B.C. to honor the god Triton. The vane featured the head and torso of a man attached to a fish's tail, and is thought to have been from 4 to 8 feet long.

The Vikings used bronze weather vanes on their ships in the ninth century, and about that time the pope reportedly decreed that every church in Europe should have a rooster on its steeple as a reminder of Luke 22:34, which states that a cock would crow after the disciple Peter had denounced Jesus three times. You'll still see roosters on weather vanes today.

Weather Vanes As Collectibles

Before 1850, weather vanes were produced by hand. But growing interest in the devices brought about factory production to meet the demand. Most of the major weather vane producers went out of business during the Great Depression, but their products are in demand today as highly sought-after collectibles.

In the digital age, the weather vane has been combined with the anemometer in an instrument called the aerovane, which looks rather like an airplane with no wings. The propeller part measures the wind speed, while the tail keeps the unit pointing into the wind, indicating which way it's blowing. Data on wind velocity and direction are constantly fed to a display unit and recording station.

GAUGING RAINFALL

The rain gauge is another important tool in the meteorologist's array of instruments. A modern gauge consists of an outer cylinder, a measuring tube that can record as little as a hundredth of an inch of rain, and a funnel. The gauge can directly measure up to 2 inches of rain; when more than that falls, the extra water flows into the outer cylinder. The observer then pours the excess from the outer cylinder back into the measuring tube to determine the total rainfall amount.

If Found, Please Return

If you find a radiosonde, send it back to the National Weather Service for reconditioning (instructions for returning it are printed on its side) to save the Weather Service the cost of a new unit. Currently only about 20 percent of the approximately 75,000 radiosondes released each year are found and returned to the NWS.

Another kind of rain gauge is the tipping bucket type, which tips and empties itself when it has accumulated 0.01 inches of rain. Immediately another bucket moves into place to continue recording rainfall, and an electronic signal is sent to a recording unit. Rainfall is measured by adding up the number of tips in a given period and multiplying by 0.01. The advantages are obvious: no one has to go outside and empty the gauge each day, and there is no water lost to evaporation. In a downpour, however, the tipping bucket gauge may not be able to empty fast enough, so its readings can be inaccurate.

RADIOSONDES: MEASUREMENTS UP IN THE AIR

Weather scientists need to know what is happening up in the atmosphere. To discover this, they attach an instrument package to a balloon and send it up. The instrument package, called a radiosonde, contains sensors that measure temperature, pressure, and relative humidity. Radiosondes and balloons have been used for decades, and were vital tools in the study and prediction of weather during World War II. The National Weather Service (NWS) is undertaking a program to replace its older radiosondes with new units that employ Global Positioning System (GPS) receivers, which will be cheaper and easier to maintain and will deliver much more accurate and reliable data.

Although the balloons used to loft radiosondes haven't changed much since World War II, the units themselves have undergone several improvements. Wind speed and direction can now be determined by tracking the balloon as it rises, and additional data streams are sent down from the radiosonde to a ground station. This data is processed through a computer before being released for distribution. The balloons can ascend to a height of more than 19 miles before they pop; a parachute then gently brings the equipment to the ground so that it can be recovered and flown again.

THE ART AND SCIENCE OF FORECASTING

Increasing Accuracy

January 2000 had already been an especially snowy month for the residents of Raleigh, North Carolina. Accustomed to an average yearly snowfall of 2 to 4 inches, the city had already seen an accumulation of more than 3 inches of snow by the twenty-third of January. That afternoon, the forecast called for an additional 1 to 2 inches that evening.

By midnight, with snow falling steadily, the forecast was 4 to 6 inches by morning, but after dawn residents of Raleigh awoke to find a startling 20 inches of powdery frozen precipitation on the ground. With thousands of people trapped in their homes and even interstate highways impassable, the governor declared a state of emergency. The North Carolina Department of Transportation's small fleet of snowplows was woefully inadequate to remove the record accumulation, which shattered a 107-year-old record.

How could a forecast go so spectacularly wrong, especially with the powerful computers and technology now available? There are some very good reasons, but they are complex. Fully understanding them requires an appreciation of how the art and science of weather forecasting has evolved and why it's still an inexact science.

HOMESPUN FORECASTING

Figuring out what the weather is going to do next has always been a challenge, and before there were reliable instruments to predict future conditions, weather watchers relied on nature for clues. Changes in animals and plants, as well as signs in the sky, were often used to predict coming weather, and very often this folksy weather wisdom had some basis in fact.

When early American settlers noticed that birds were going to roost early, they knew that rain or snow was approaching. They also watched flowers such as dandelions, which fold their petals before a storm. If night brought a halo around the Moon, rain was expected. (Now we know that a lunar halo is caused by light shining through the ice crystals of cirrus or cirrostratus clouds that often precede thunderstorms.)

Caterpillars As Meteorologists

For generations, country folk have relied on the woolly bear caterpillar (sometimes called the woolly worm) for their winter weather forecasts. According to legend, the little black-and-brown caterpillar can predict the severity of the coming winter by the width of its bands: the wider the brown segment, the milder the winter.

Just as modern forecasters can't boast of a 100 percent success rate in their forecasts, folk wisdom often got it wrong. Have you ever heard that "lightning never strikes twice in the same place"? Tell that to the workers in the Empire State Building, which gets hit about twenty-three times a year, on average. In fact, during one especially bad thunderstorm it was struck eight times in twenty-four minutes.

PRETECH TROUBLES

After the development of weather instruments, forecasting became much more accurate. But as late as the mid-1950s, incoming weather data were assembled and plotted on charts by hand. In many cases forecasts were based on historical records that were compared with current conditions for similarities. Often the results were surprisingly accurate, but human brains were just not up to the task of quickly analyzing the huge quantities of data that were needed to consistently generate accurate forecasts.

CRUNCHING NUMBERS

In 1943, with most scientific resources being directed toward the war effort, scientists at the Moore School of Electrical Engineering at the University of Pennsylvania began construction on a machine that would, quite literally, change the world.

Dubbed ENIAC (Electronic Numerical Integrator and Computer), the groundbreaking device was designed to compute the trajectories of ballistic artillery shells. ENIAC was a behemoth by today's standards, containing 18,000 vacuum tubes (which broke down at the average rate of one every seven minutes) and 1,500 relay switches. It weighed in at a hefty 30 tons, and could compute fourteen 10-digit multiplications per second. Operators used 6,000 switches and a host of jumper cables to program the beast.

In 1946, while using ENIAC to simulate nuclear explosions, Princeton mathematician John von Neumann realized that the computer might also be used for weather prediction. In 1950 his team produced the first computer-based numerical weather forecast, and while it wasn't an unqualified success, it did show that numerical forecasting was feasible.

Although the house-sized ENIAC was much faster than manual calculations, those early electronic pioneers learned that atmospheric conditions change more rapidly than the early machines could calculate them. The sheer volume of data meant that there was still much room, and need, for improvement.

In 1954, elements of the Navy, Air Force, and Weather Bureau formed the Joint Numerical Weather Prediction Unit in Suitland, Maryland, to further refine numerical forecasting, and in 1955 the unit began issuing regular real-time forecasts. Still, computerized forecasts were not as accurate as the older subjective methods.

SATELLITES: METEOROLOGY'S EYES IN THE SKY

While computer makers toiled to create faster processors, the science of weather observation and forecasting was about to take its next giant leap. In 1946, with Hitler's V2 rocket attacks on London still a fresh wound, the Army Air Forces and the RAND Corporation cosponsored a paper entitled "Preliminary Design of an Experimental World-Circling Spaceship." Though mostly concerned with military surveillance, the paper mentioned that such a satellite might also make a good weather reconnaissance platform.

In 1954 the first pictures of a tropical storm were taken from space using a US Navy Aerobee rocket. The spectacular photos galvanized the meteorological community: for the first time a giant weather system could be seen in its entirety. But rockets took time to prepare for launch, were expensive and difficult to recover, and spent very little time over their targets. What was really needed was an observation platform that could stay in space for long periods of time, and the World-Circling Spaceship was it.

Failure to Launch

NASA had its hands full just getting TIROS 1 off the ground. While still in the planning stages, the satellite went through a succession of proposed launch vehicles until the Thor-Able rocket (a modified intercontinental ballistic missile) was chosen. The first Thor-Able blew up 146 seconds after launch, and the first prototype TIROS spun out of control after reaching orbit.

On April 1, 1960, the recently formed National Aeronautics and Space Administration (NASA) launched the world's first weather satellite atop an Air Force Thor-Able rocket. Weighing only 263 pounds, TIROS 1 (Television and Infrared Observation Satellite) began to return dozens of pictures of the earth and its cloud cover on its very first day in orbit. Though grainy, those first crude pictures were a snapshot of the future for weather forecasters, who for the first time had an eye in the sky for tracking weather systems like fronts and hurricanes. Orbiting the planet every ninety-nine minutes, TIROS 1 spotted a tropical cyclone in the waters of the South Pacific north of New Zealand nine days after launch, the first storm to be detected by satellite. Until that time, tropical storm prediction relied on ship and aircraft reports that were often spotty and unreliable.

GOES to Show You

Today NOAA operates two satellites called GOES (Geostationary Operational Environmental Satellites); one keeps an eye on weather conditions in North and South America and most of the Atlantic Ocean, and the other monitors part of North America and the Pacific Ocean. Geosynchronous satellites provide an overview of a whole hemisphere's weather conditions since they are capable of imaging the full disk of Earth in one snapshot.

GOES satellites sport two main instruments called an imager and a sounder. The imager measures the amount of energy being radiated from the earth and how much solar energy is being reflected from the surface and atmosphere. The sounder takes the earth's temperature and determines the atmospheric moisture level, as well as surface and cloud top temperatures and ozone levels.

GOES is also outfitted with a search-and-rescue transponder and a space environment monitor consisting of a magnetometer, an X-ray sensor, a high-energy proton and alpha detector, and an energetic particles sensor. These instruments allow GOES to report on the state of the solar wind and warn of approaching solar storms caused by CMEs (coronal mass ejections) from the Sun. That's a lot of bang for the buck considering GOES started out strictly as a weather satellite.

FORECASTING MODELS

Using Supercomputers

With more powerful satellites being launched and returning more and more data, there was a growing need for faster computers that could handle the load. Once supercomputers arrived on the scene, forecasters finally had a tool that could assemble and make sense out of the huge volume of data that could now be gathered.

DOING THE MATH

Forecasting is really educated guesswork. There are so many variables that go into a forecast, and they're always changing. To more fully understand these changes, atmospheric models with a limited set of data were developed in the early days of computing. These models attempted to describe the present state of the temperature, moisture, and pressure in the atmosphere and how those conditions change with the passage of time.

These days, a forecast is a product of six to eight mathematical equations for a given point. Information on air pressure, wind speed, humidity, air density, and the results of surface and upper-air measurements are loaded into a supercomputer, and a program is run that describes the conditions that will occur in a small unit of future time. The program analyzes data for a large number of "grid points," or imaginary squares of various sizes, both at the surface and up to eighteen layers into the atmosphere.

Now the forecaster has a prediction of future conditions for the next ten minutes or so. Using that data as a starting point, the information is fed back into the computer, which does another prediction for the next few minutes until it reaches a desired time in the future, such as twelve, twenty-four, or thirty-six hours from the starting point. The computer can now draw a map called a prognostic chart that shows how all of the lows, highs, and other weather factors will appear at a future time.

As computer models are developed, their accuracy is tracked and small adjustments are made to improve them. Because one model may evolve to be better at forecasting surface low-pressure systems, while another excels at predicting the movement of upper-level air, meteorologists can pick and choose among the many models available, selecting the ones that are more likely to result in a correct forecast.

TRUE GRIDS

Because computer modeling is accomplished using grid points, and a forecast is drawn using conditions within each grid box, it follows that the smaller the grid the more accurate the forecast will be. Global climate models work with a grid that's about 300 miles square (larger than the state of Iowa). Because it's a three-dimensional box that extends into the upper levels of the atmosphere, with data being plotted at each level, the output of just one grid computation can total hundreds of megabytes of data. As grids become smaller, the data analysis and storage requirements rise exponentially, and so grids smaller than 300 miles square contain too much data for the purposes of global modeling. As a result, global models are still much less accurate than regional ones, although they're useful in determining large-scale climate changes over time.

Regional grids produce more accurate forecasts than the global variety, but because they're smaller, they're dependable only for a short period; weather from adjacent grids always intrudes before too long.

Although computers are great tools for aiding in the creation of weather forecasts, human interpreters still need to analyze the output from computer models, compare them with past data that have been gathered over a long time period, and determine what changes will improve the model's accuracy. There is simply no substitute for human experience and wisdom.

Climate models depend on a detailed description of a grid point for their accuracy, so each area is modeled differently depending on whether it's over land, ice, or ocean. Land specialists help build models that incorporate topographic features like mountains and rivers, as well as water runoff on the surface and the amount of water in the soil. The models also include forests and other areas of vegetation, because plants reflect less sunlight than land and the amount of carbon dioxide that plants release can affect local air composition.

Oceanographers are called on to use their knowledge of the sea to input factors such as salt content, freshwater runoff, sea ice, ocean temperature, and density into numerical models. Atmospheric scientists input information on the distribution of gases in the air, how solar radiation is affecting air temperatures, and the amount of pollutants like industrial smoke and automobile emissions.

DISORDERLY MODELS

With high-tech teamwork and speedy supercomputers combining to create forecasts, why aren't at least short-term forecasts more dependable? The answer lies in the tendency for small atmospheric disturbances to be greatly magnified over time. Meteorologist Edward Lorenz discovered this effect, called chaos theory, in 1963. Lorenz was running a weather-modeling computer program accurate to the sixth decimal place, but after running into a problem, he reentered the data using a printout, which rounded to three decimals. To his great surprise, the extremely small difference of missing the last three decimal places resulted in a very different processing run.

Utter Chaos

Lorenz described chaos theory as "a system that has two states that look the same on separate occasions, but can develop into states that are noticeably different." A golf ball dropped from the same height above a fixed point would always land on the same spot, he noted, but a piece of paper would not because during its fall it would be acted on by chaotic forces like air movement. Because those forces changed constantly, the path of the paper to the ground could not be predicted with any degree of accuracy.

The Butterfly Effect

Lorenz illustrated chaos theory by concocting the "butterfly effect," which states that the flapping of a butterfly's wings in China could cause tiny atmospheric changes that over a period of time could affect weather patterns in New York City.

It's What You Put Into It

Computer models are only a simulation of the atmosphere; they make assumptions about weather conditions that may or may not be accurate. Even though great pains are taken to eliminate models that don't perform well, they are not now, nor will they ever be, perfect. Another problem is inherent in regional models: errors creep in along their boundaries as weather from nearby grids sneaks in.

With the advent of satellites and radiosondes, many more observation points are now available than in the past, and forecasts have improved as a result. But because of the computational requirements of smaller grids, most models still use data points that are too far apart to accurately predict the movement of small-scale weather systems like thunderstorms. In addition, many models don't take land features like hills and lakes into account, thereby introducing that first small error that Lorenz showed can be magnified over time into one giant boo-boo.

A NEW HOPE

When you take the effects of chaos into account, is there any real hope that forecasts—especially long-range ones—can be improved? Actually, it's already happening. Ensemble forecasting combines several computational models into one, using a weighted average system. Introducing different weather factors into a model at the outset mimics the effects of chaos, and often results in a more accurate result. Running several of these ensemble models while using a slightly different weight factor each time increases the chances of at least one being correct, and by weeding out the ones that don't work, forecasts can become much more dependable.

Another way that scientists are improving forecasts is by filling in data gaps that have long existed in certain remote parts of the globe. In much of the Southern Hemisphere, for example, which is mostly covered by vast oceans, gathering atmospheric information in real time has been a challenge. Now a NASA scatterometer, which is able to measure wind speeds from orbit, passes over 90 percent of the world's oceans each day, greatly improving marine forecasts.

Faith in Forecasting

Forecasters compare the output of different models and assign a degree of confidence in each one depending on how much faith they have in a particular forecast. In general the more the models disagree, the less predictable the weather is.

Recently, it was discovered that some areas of the earth's surface are responsible for more chaos errors than others, and were dubbed "chaos hot spots." These areas, which cover about 20 percent of the earth's surface, are now the target of intense observation since they seem to cause most of the inaccuracies in current global forecasts. As scientists move from the global to the regional and even local scale, more hot spots will be identified, and forecasts for those areas will improve.

Researchers are now comparing computer models with historical conditions. They feed climatic information for a certain past day into the system and then run a projection of the weather for the next fifteen or thirty days. Comparing the results of the projection with the actual conditions that occurred in the past can demonstrate the accuracy of a model.

With the realization that a small atmospheric eddy in one country can affect the weather in another, in 1992 the World Meteorological Organization (WMO) began a program called the Global Climate

Observing System (GCOS). GCOS was designed to improve forecasts by coordinating weather data from all over the globe.

POWER TO THE PROGNOSTICATORS

Of course one way to improve forecasts is to throw more computing power at them, and that's just what IBM is doing with its Deep Thunder project. Using the same type of supercomputer as Deep Blue, the system used to defeat Russian chess master Garry Kasparov in May 1997, the company is hoping to substantially reduce the size of a weather modeling grid and produce a much more accurate local forecast. IBM is currently issuing a daily forecast for New York City using Deep Thunder, creating complex 3-D images that can give forecasters a snapshot of future weather conditions at a glance.

While improved forecasts will help you refine everyday activities, such as avoiding a cloudy day at the beach and letting you know when to bring an umbrella to work, these improvements hold enormous implications for businesses. It's been estimated that in the airline industry alone, weather-related problems cost up to $269 million a year, and improvements in forecasting can help them reduce these costs. Even power companies lose money when bad forecasts cause them to overproduce electricity. The better the forecasts, the more efficiently they can produce the power we depend on.

Even more important, accurate and timely forecasts can save lives and money. In 2016, fifteen weather-related disasters cost more than $1 billion each. Clearly, every small step in improving weather prediction is welcome, especially when that weather turns violent.

LIGHTNING

Fire in the Sky

The most common type of lightning is the cloud-to-cloud type; only about 20 percent of all lightning strikes are directed toward the ground. But the cloud-to-ground variety is the one that affects people more often, so it receives the most study.

Fulgurites

When lightning strikes sand or certain rock, the heat immediately melts and fuses the material it encounters, creating long underground glass tubes called fulgurites. These channels are usually from 0.5 to 2 inches across and can burrow as far as 20 yards into the ground. Fulgurites are fragile, and because they are difficult to remove from the soil, large specimens are rare.

HOW LIGHTNING IS CREATED

For lightning to occur, there have to be areas of opposite electrical charges within a cumulonimbus cloud. How those regions develop and why they separate is an undiscovered secret, but one theory says that the collisions between small hailstones and ice crystals within a storm cause a positive charge in the upper regions while the lower and middle parts of the cloud gain a negative charge due to the influence of downdrafts and gravity.

Because unlike charges attract each other, the ground below the thunderstorm becomes positively charged, and as the cloud moves it drags this area of positive charge behind it. The resulting electrical field continues to build, but because the air between the cloud and the ground acts as an insulator, no current flows between them. If you measured the positive charges under the storm at this point (not recommended!), you'd find that protruding structures like radio towers, church steeples, and stubborn golfers have a stronger charge than the ground, making them a much more likely target for lightning.

Eventually this charge becomes so powerful that it overcomes the air's insulating effect, and a bolt of lightning zaps out of the cloud. It's over in less than a second, but in that time as many as ten separate lightning strokes can be generated. The fact that it looks like one continuous streak is because the human eye can't register the distinct pulses fast enough; instead of separate flashes, your retinas see a flickering effect, because each pulse lasts only a few millionths of a second.

Looking at Lightning in Slo-Mo

Lightning is very difficult to study. Not only is it extremely short-lived, but nobody wants to get too close to a billion volts of electricity. Imagine for a moment that you could slow down the passage of time, so that microseconds lasted for minutes. You'd be able to clearly see each phase of a lightning bolt as it developed, and what you saw would probably surprise you.

The first thing you'd see in a cloud-to-ground flash is a barely visible streamer of lightning, called a stepped leader, emerging from the cloud. The stepped leader travels the distance of about a city block in a microsecond and then pauses for up to fifty microseconds to decide where to go next. If there's a stronger electrical field in a different direction, the leader will change course and head toward it, creating a crooked appearance. This stop-and-start process continues until the leader gets close to the ground, when it will often branch into several forks.

As it gets closer to the ground, the leader induces a rapid increase in the strength of electrical fields on the ground (around ten million volts' worth), especially in taller objects. Suddenly another bolt of lightning jumps from the ground up toward the stepped leader, completing a cloud/ground electrical circuit.

Although the stepped leader had to go through the trial-and-error process of finding the best path to the ground, the return stroke doesn't have that limitation. Taking advantage of its prefab pathway, it leaps back toward the cloud with a flash as bright as a million light bulbs, making the trip all the way up to the cloud and back down as many as ten times in a fraction of a second.

The Big Flash-Bang

The pencil-thin bolt instantly heats the air in this corridor to 54,000°F—hotter than the surface of the Sun—and since heated air expands, a shock wave explodes outward from the lightning channel at the speed of sound, creating a blast of thunder. The bright flash caused by the bolt is expanding outward too, but at the speed of light (186,000 miles per second), a million times faster than the thunder. The flash reaches us almost instantly, while the thunderclap moseys along toward our eardrums at a leisurely 1,125 feet per second or so. If the lightning strike is more than about 15 miles away, you probably won't hear the thunder, since sound waves generally curve upward around thunderstorms.

Most often there will be at least four distinct bolts traveling through the channel before the strike is over. Stepped leaders that form after the first one are called dart leaders, and they're usually less powerful than the initial bolt. Dart leaders that depart from the original channel on their way back to the ground will give the lightning stroke a forked appearance. If the wind blows the lightning channel sideways at high speed, ribbon lightning results. It is as if the moving corridor creates a luminous strip in the air.

Keep Your Distance

Just because you're quite a distance from a thunderstorm doesn't mean you should let your guard down. Cumulonimbus clouds can spawn "positive giants": lightning strikes that come from the storm's anvil-shaped head and can blast outward for up to 20 miles.

SHOCKING VARIANTS

Other forms of lightning include heat lightning, which is just ordinary lightning seen from a great distance, and sheet lightning, which is lightning striking within a cloud or from one cloud to another. When the actual bolt is obscured by the cloud, it lights up the entire structure, momentarily making it look like a huge white sheet.

Sometimes the positive charge that accumulates on flagpoles, ship masts, and other high points doesn't provoke a lightning strike, but instead appears as a halo of sparks or a weird glow around the top of the object. That's called St. Elmo's fire, named after the patron saint of mariners. The effect is caused by charged plasma called a corona discharge and is similar to the glow given off by a fluorescent light.

Don't Catch This Ball

St. Elmo's fire isn't really lightning, but at least the basic electrical phenomenon that causes it is understood. Not so with the phenomenon of ball lightning, which continues to confound scientists. About as far from split-a-tree-in-your-backyard lightning as you can get, ball lightning is a true original. Although it has never been photographed, so many people have reported seeing the phenomenon that there's little doubt of its existence.

Most observers describe ball lightning as a luminous red, orange, or yellow sphere floating along in the air a few yards or less from the ground, often near a thunderstorm. Some people hear a hissing sound or smell an odor like ozone. The spheres range in size from a few inches to a few feet, although most are in the 4- to 8-inch category and last only a few seconds.

Theories on the nature of ball lightning are a dime a dozen, ranging from plasma suspended in a magnetic field to swamp gas ignited by a lightning strike. One recent theory supposes that when lightning strikes certain types of soils, the ground can vaporize, creating hot gases that "burp" out of the soil and then condense into tiny, electricity-conducting wires that form a glowing sphere.

SPRITES, ELVES, AND BLUE JETS

Exotic Lightning

Recently even more exotic forms of lightning have been discovered above thunderstorms. Faint flickers of light from the tops of storms had been reported for more than a century—some observers said it looked as though the tops of clouds were on fire—but verification was difficult until the right instruments were developed. In fact some Air Force pilots had seen the phenomenon for years but were reluctant to report lightning that went the "wrong" way. In 1989 researchers videotaped a pulse of light leaping from the top of a thunderstorm toward the heavens. With no idea what they were seeing, they dubbed it a sprite.

SNAPSHOT OF A SPRITE

In 1994 a group of scientists from the University of Minnesota in a high-flying NASA jet were testing a low-light camera normally used to image the aurora borealis. While orbiting high over a thunderstorm, they pointed the camera at the distant horizon and quite accidentally captured the first color images of a sprite. The pictures revealed a large red puff rising from the storm, appearing just as a powerful lightning bolt exploded below. The sprite, which had a surprisingly delicate structure, rose some 60 miles toward space before dissipating.

What could account for the existence of something that looked like a huge red jellyfish high in the atmosphere? That's still being debated, but scientists do know a few things about sprites:

Top: Aristotle was one of the first people to systematically study the weather and try to understand what caused different kinds of weather. Although his understanding of natural science was limited—he thought there were only four elements: earth, wind, air, and fire (in fact, there are 118)—he did correctly conclude that the Sun could put air masses into motion (resulting in wind), and that clouds were condensed water vapor.

Photo Credit: © Getty Images/denisk0

NAPOLEON IN RUSSIA.

Bottom: In 1812, when the Emperor Napoleon of France invaded Russia, weather came to the aid of his enemies and played a significant role in his defeat. The Russians drew back before him, destroying food stocks in the process. He reached Moscow in September and remained in the Russian capital for five weeks before beginning the return to France. Winter set in and the French soldiers, without proper clothing, walked in snow up to their knees. Half the French army froze to death or died of weather-related illnesses.

Photo Credit: © Getty Images/benoitb

Top: Cumulus clouds are among the most common kinds of clouds; they're puffy with flat bottoms. They often give rise to cumulonimbus clouds, which are much larger and taller and are more likely to bring rain or snow. **Bottom:** If the Sun is shining while there are a lot of water droplets in the sky, the droplets refract, reflect, and disperse the white light of the Sun into its various component colors. The result is a rainbow. In some rare instances, fog rather than rain can produce a rainbow; the water particles in the fog are so small that the rainbow appears white.

Photo Credits: © Getty Images/skyhobo and 123RF/Jaroslav Machacek

Top: Supercells start as ordinary thunderstorms, but because of winds blowing at different speeds at different levels of the atmosphere, the storm tilts, pushing out the colder air and allowing warm air to rush in. The result is winds moving up to 150 miles per hour. In this picture a supercell is beginning to form. **Bottom:** If snowfall is accompanied by winds of more than 35 mph and visibility is down to a quarter mile or less, the snowstorm has officially become a blizzard. The Blizzard of 1978 that hit New England closed much of Boston for ten days.

Photo Credits: © Getty Images/Minerva Studio and Getty Images/DenisTangneyJr

The Tacoma Narrows Bridge, spanning the Puget Sound south of Seattle, was completed in July 1940. Four months later, it collapsed as a result of an aeroelastic flutter, a sudden instability caused by 40-mile-an-hour wind gusts. Although no people were killed, the disaster led to radical changes in the way bridges are designed to avoid such accidents in the future.

Photo Credit: © Wikimedia Commons/Stillman Fires Collection

Lightning, an electrical discharge during a thunderstorm, is caused by the upper part of the cloud becoming positively charged while the middle and lower parts of the cloud are negative. It's the reaction between these parts of the cloud that results in the lightning. Most lightning bolts are isolated, but during especially severe storms, multiple bolts can occur almost simultaneously.

Photo Credit: © Getty Images/shaunl

Top: Floods can occur when the ground is so soaked that it is unable to absorb water or when the ground is so dry that water can't penetrate it. Flooding also happens when rivers or lakes overrun their boundaries. Each year, floods cause millions of dollars in damage and many deaths across the globe. **Bottom:** Droughts can damage the ecosystem and cause wildfires that burn millions of acres.

Photo Credits: © Getty Images/SlobodonMiljevic and Getty Images/mack2happy

The peak of the Atlantic hurricane season is in September and October. During that time, large masses of humid air over warm waters form tropical storms. If one of these strengthens and starts to rotate, it can become a hurricane. Such storms in the Atlantic and northeast Pacific are called hurricanes; similar storms that form in the southern Pacific are called typhoons.

Photo Credit: © Getty Images/Harvepino

An undersea earthquake is one of many events that can create a tsunami—a wave that can overwhelm everything in its path. A tsunami's size depends on the depth of the water where the event occurs, the violence of the event that caused it, and the distance the wave has to travel to reach land. Large tsunamis that strike populated areas can be deadly. In 2004, an earthquake in the Indian Ocean created a tsunami that killed more than 280,000 people.

Photo Credit: © Getty Images/Zacarias Pereira Da Mata

Hurricane Katrina struck the Gulf Coast in August 2005. By the time it was over, 80 percent of New Orleans was flooded; levees and floodwalls had been breached; and more than 700 people in New Orleans were killed. Many of the houses in poorer districts were entirely destroyed by wind and water.

Photo Credit: © Getty Images/ ParkerDeen

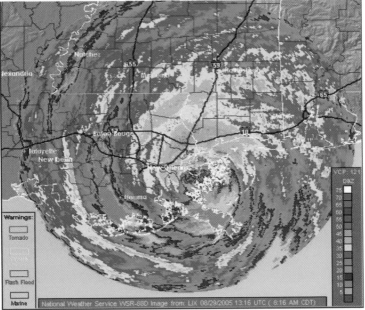

The development of radar during World War II was a watershed for weather forecasting since it showed the direction and velocity of moving air masses. In this radar image of Hurricane Katrina as it struck the Gulf Coast in 2005, the center of the storm is passing over the greater New Orleans area.

Photo Credit: © National Weather Service/Public Domain

- They appear only during very large thunderstorms.
- They're usually brightest about 40 miles up in the atmosphere.
- They last only about ten milliseconds.
- They appear only after reverse, or positive, cloud-to-ground lightning.
- They almost always appear in groups.

Elves and Blue Jets

With the discovery of sprites, many more observers turned their attention to the lofty heights of severe thunderstorms, and soon some other strange effects were discovered. Narrow beams of blue light were spotted over some clouds. Named blue jets by their discoverers, these narrow cone-shaped columns seem to leap from the top of a thunderstorm and soar high into the stratosphere at more than 300 times the speed of sound. Although they're much rarer than sprites, blue jets are a bit more long-lived; they are visible to the naked eye at night.

Shortly after the discovery of blue jets, scientists at Stanford University announced that they had spotted an even stranger light in the heavens: a red halo that seemed to do the impossible by propagating outward from a thunderstorm to an altitude of about 40 to 60 miles high at a velocity faster than the speed of light. But it wasn't yet time for Einstein to roll over in his grave; further research showed that no single particle was moving that fast. The phenomenon, dubbed "elves," was caused by air molecules firing in rapid sequence after being stimulated by the lightning pulse, like chase lights around a movie marquee. Their causes are still being investigated.

One theory on the origin of elves says that the electromagnetic pulse caused by a lightning strike can rise and expand through the cloud like a balloon, finally breaking free above the storm, where it causes charged particles to glow red. Others say they could be caused by storm-produced gamma rays that were recently detected by NASA's Compton Gamma Ray Observatory satellite.

BOLTS, BLAZES, AND BLACKOUTS

Each year, lightning starts around 10,000 forest fires in the United States alone, laying waste to more than $50 million worth of timber. The National Lightning Safety Institute estimates that the total cost of lightning strikes, including damage to both property and people, may total upward of $4 billion to $5 billion per year. A strike near your home can shred your trees, shut off your power, and cook your appliances. A large, well-placed bolt can knock out power to an entire city.

Blackout Protection

Brownouts and blackouts can wreak havoc with your electronic devices, and a lightning strike can destroy them. A surge protector for each device is imperative, but an even better bet is an uninterruptible power supply (UPS), which can allow you to shut your computer down after a power problem without losing data.

On the night of July 13, 1977, a line of thunderstorms formed to the north of New York City. The sound of air conditioners running at full blast nearly drowned out their rumble as New Yorkers sought relief from the heat. Shortly after 8:30, powerful lightning strikes hit two high-voltage power lines, starting a chain of events that knocked out the city's power grid and plunged the Big Apple into darkness. During what became known as the Night of Terror, 3,776 people were arrested for looting and other crimes, and the fire department fought 1,037 blazes. One Bronx dealership was robbed of fifty cars in a single evening. Thousands were trapped in darkened elevators and subway cars. Both Kennedy International and LaGuardia Airports were closed, and hospitals were forced to resort to emergency generators for power.

With so much at stake, the federal government assisted in financing a national lightning data service that eventually grew into the National Lightning Detection Network (NLDN). Consisting of a web of magnetic direction finders scattered across the country, the NLDN can instantly triangulate the location of a cloud-to-ground lightning strike and transmit that information to the Network Control Center, where it appears on an electronic map of the United States. Warnings can now be issued for storms with especially violent electrical activity.

TAMING LIGHTNING

Dr. Franklin Invents a Rod

Satellite observation has shown that there are more than one hundred flashes of lightning per second all over the globe. That translates to more than three million bolts blasting from the more than 40,000 thunderstorms that dot the planet each day. Lightning kills about one hundred Americans each year—more than any other kind of severe weather except floods—yet many of its secrets still remain undiscovered.

THE FIRST LIGHTNING ROD WAS NAMED BEN

A bolt of lightning is really just a giant spark that discharges pent-up electrical energy from a cloud into the ground, or from one cloud to another. In Benjamin Franklin's day, charges created by static electricity were already being stored in containers called Leyden jars, a primitive form of capacitor. Lightning wasn't yet linked with electricity, although Franklin suspected a connection between the two.

Franklin had designed an experiment to prove his theory using what he called a sentry box, but construction delays caused him to set it aside in favor of a kite with a conductive string. Near the end of the string, he tied a key. To this key he also tied a short length of nonconducting silk cord. His plan was to hold the silk cord with one hand while holding his other hand near the key. Franklin theorized that when lightning struck the kite, a spark would jump from the key to his knuckles.

In 1752, during a Pennsylvania thunderstorm, the most famous kite in history took to the air. Sure enough, a lightning bolt hit the kite and immediately sparks flew from the key to Franklin's hand, proving once and for all that lightning was indeed an electrical phenomenon. It seems a miracle that he wasn't killed on the spot.

Follow-Up and Disaster

The year after Franklin's kite flight, Swedish physicist G.W. Richmann, who had read about Franklin's earlier experiment, constructed a sentry box of his own. Following Franklin's instructions to the letter, he stood in the box during a lightning storm. He was rewarded with a direct strike, which killed him instantly. The moral: don't try this at home, or anywhere else.

Franklin also invented the lightning rod after discovering that an electrical charge could be drained away via a conducting rod buried in the ground. Eventually, he came up with the idea of putting the rod on a rooftop and connecting it to a wire to transfer the energy of a lightning bolt directly into the soil, sparing the building from harm. Lightning rods don't "attract" lightning, they just give it a harmless path to take into the ground, which is all it really wants in the first place.

WHY WE HAVE FLOODS

Waters on the Rise

Flash floods remain difficult to predict because they're a result of rapidly changing conditions. They can be caused not only by sudden cloudbursts but also by quickly melting snow or ice and the collapse of natural or manmade dams. The seeds of disaster can be sown on what seems to be a perfect day.

Floods caused by several days of rainfall or melting snow give plenty of notice, but their effects can be much more damaging and widespread. Many rivers flood on a regular basis and have done so for centuries, but people nonetheless build homes on their banks and floodplains, placing themselves directly in harm's way. Loss of lives and property is an inevitable outcome—another reason why floods are America's number one weather-related killers.

A Disaster Named Katrina

When Hurricane Katrina hit the Gulf Coast in August 2005, it smashed many of the levees that protected New Orleans. More than fifty breaches were reported and floodwaters rushed into large parts of the city. Later investigations concluded that the levees might have held (or at least held better) if they had been inspected and repaired regularly. In the years after the storm, many of the levees were rebuilt, this time with materials and designs aimed at withstanding a similar event.

Population growth calls for more housing. With wetlands being drained for developments, rivers being channeled, and levees being built, flooding rivers will crest at a higher elevation. Urban development covers large areas with pavement and concrete, so water that was once able to soak into the ground over time now rushes directly into streams and rivers. When you throw an approaching hurricane or tropical storm into the mix, it's time to look for higher ground.

One pattern meteorologists look for in a developing flash flood is where storms with heavy rainfall linger. Storms may hover over one area for hours, or they may move in such a way that a continuous line of storm cells passes repeatedly over the same spot in a pattern called training. They also watch out for backbuilding, which occurs when a storm is able to regenerate itself on its back edge as quickly as it moves forward. When this happens, one small area can receive catastrophic amounts of rain in a short time.

THE DANGER OF DROUGHTS

Agricultural Disasters

As damaging as too much water can be, too little can cause just as much trouble. When an area doesn't receive enough rain for an extended period of time, drought conditions result. It may seem strange but when eastern North Carolina was drowning under Hurricane Floyd's floodwaters in 1999, the western part of the state was suffering from a severe drought.

The Ripple Effect

When a drought occurs in a food-producing area, its impact can extend far beyond the local region. With farmers and agribusinesses losing money and the price of food and timber on the rise, unemployment levels increase, foreclosures become common, and cities and states receive less tax money.

Most droughts result from fluctuations in large-scale circulation patterns in the atmosphere, and they can be directly influenced by the location of high-pressure systems. When large rotating air masses get cut off from the standard airflow moving from west to east across the country, they linger in one place and can block the progress of advancing weather systems, introducing a wholesale change in climate. If these atmospheric roadblocks last for extended periods of time, floods, drought, freezes, and heat waves often become the rule.

DUST IN THE WIND

Sometimes the effects of a drought can be amplified by human activity. In the 1930s the Great Plains of the United States began to experience droughts. For years settlers in the region had been planting wheat and harvesting bountiful crops, but when the dry conditions arrived, they kept on planting and plowing in spite of the diminishing rainfall. With the native grasses mostly gone, high winds whipped huge clouds of dust and soil into the air, in some cases completely burying homes and automobiles in heaps of drifting soil. By May 1934, a cloud of topsoil from the Great Plains blanketed the eastern United States for a distance of some 1,500 miles.

No one who saw it ever forgot the black blizzard (Black Sunday) that occurred on Palm Sunday of 1935. Eyewitnesses described it as a beautiful, peaceful day until late afternoon, when flocks of birds appeared on the horizon, fleeing for their lives. Behind them came a black wall of dust rising 7,000 feet into the air, engulfing everything in its path. With the morning's weather so calm, many people had taken to the roads for leisurely day trips, but as the dust storm engulfed them, motorists collided with each other in the choking darkness, unable to see more than a foot or two ahead. The grit generated so much static electricity as it swirled over the highways that automobile electrical systems shorted out, stalling engines and stranding many drivers in the storm.

Taking refuge indoors, homeowners stuffed rags, sheets, and clothing into cracks under doors and around windows, but the dust got in anyway, coating everything inside with a thick layer of black dirt.

The next day Robert Geiger, a correspondent for the *Washington Evening Star*, would name the ongoing drought the Dust Bowl. It lasted for nearly a decade and excavated an estimated 850 million tons of soil from the Great Plains.

FORECASTING DROUGHTS

Droughts are difficult to predict because they're always the end result of many causative factors. Because they develop much more slowly than floods, droughts often aren't identified until they're already under way. Adding to the confusion, there are different ways of measuring droughts:

- **Meteorological**—How much the precipitation amounts differ from normal. Because not every area gets the same amount of rainfall, a drought in one place might not be considered a drought in another.
- **Agricultural**—The amount of moisture in the soil is no longer sufficient to grow a particular crop.
- **Hydrological**—Both surface and underground water supplies are below normal.
- **Socioeconomic**—A lack of water begins to affect people's daily lives.

NOAA researchers examining tree rings and other indicators of historical droughts are learning that large-scale dry weather events tend to occur on a regular basis. Their findings may eventually lead to better ways of forecasting droughts. The bad news is that disasters like the Dust Bowl may not be all that unusual on a climatological scale. More severe and longer-lasting droughts could occur at any time. History indicates that the United States might expect a

Dust Bowl–sized drought once or twice each century, and that past droughts have been much worse than more recent ones.

The scientists found that during the last half of the sixteenth century there was a "megadrought" in the western United States that was the most severe and persistent in the past 1,000 to 2,000 years. The scientists concluded that future droughts might be even worse due to the effects of global warming. With the population growth exploding, the economic effects could be catastrophic.

Better Predictions

As more is learned about the conditions that precede a drought, efforts at prediction have improved considerably. With the El Niño/La Niña pattern now identified and successfully forecast, meteorologists are getting better at making the connection between large-scale recurring weather patterns and how they cause droughts, flooding, and other natural disasters.

HURRICANES

Mother Nature's Fury

The skipper he stood beside the helm,

His pipe was in his mouth,

And he watched how the veering flaw did blow

The smoke now West, now South.

Then up and spake an old Sailòr,

Had sailed to the Spanish Main,

"I pray thee, put into yonder port,

For I fear a hurricane."

—From "The Wreck of the Hesperus," by Henry Wadsworth Longfellow

---

It seems inconceivable that something so large and deadly could possibly have a beneficial side. But hurricanes are really just giant heat engines that pick up warmth from the oceans in the warmer latitudes and transport it to the colder climates, helping to balance the earth's warm and cool zones.

Born in the Tropics

Tropical disturbances often form when stormy weather over Africa moves off-shore near the Cape Verde islands and begins to make its way east across the Atlantic. During the peak of the Atlantic hurricane season in September and October, some of the largest and most dangerous hurricanes form in this region.

HOW AND WHERE HURRICANES FORM

When ocean waters are warm, humidity is high, and winds are light, the conditions are right for a hurricane to form. The tropical Atlantic, the Caribbean, and the Gulf of Mexico provide this atmospheric mix every year from June through November. Hurricanes also need something to set them spinning, a job handled by the Coriolis force that is created by the earth's rotation. Because the Coriolis force is zero at the equator, storm systems must migrate at least 5 degrees north of it before they can pick up enough spin to become a hurricane.

Most hurricanes—about two-thirds—form between 10 and 20 degrees north latitude, along a constant feature called the Intertropical Convergence Zone, or ITCZ. This zone marks the area where northeasterly breezes meet southeasterly trade winds, causing the warm, humid tropical air to rise. As the air rises, it naturally condenses into clouds and rain, which often gather into groups of thunderstorms and move along the ITCZ from east to west.

Mixing the Ingredients

Like tornadoes, hurricanes can form only when a specific set of conditions is in place. Because they feed on heat, hurricanes need water that is at least 80°F from the surface down to a depth of about 150 feet. The atmosphere above a developing storm must be substantially cooler than the surface, allowing the system to develop towering thunderclouds. The midlevel layers of the atmosphere must be saturated with water vapor, adding to the fuel that powers the storm. As noted earlier, hurricanes can't form at the equator, so a developing storm has to be at least 500 miles away from zero latitude to get going, and there must be at least some low-level spin in the atmosphere to get it started.

Unlike tornadoes, which depend on winds blowing in different directions at varying levels of the atmosphere to get them spinning, wind shear is a hurricane's enemy. Many potential hurricanes have been ripped apart by areas of strong wind shear aloft. But once conditions are right and a low-pressure system has developed at the surface, it can become a self-sustaining atmospheric juggernaut.

Visitors from Afar

Although hurricanes usually begin in the tropics, they can wander far from their breeding grounds, bringing their own brand of mischief to northern climates. Many major hurricanes have battered New York City, and one model predicts that a Category 3 storm could cause a storm surge of 20 feet at the Statue of Liberty.

As converging winds spin toward the center of the low, they are drawn into its core and rise upward, producing an area of high pressure above the storm. Although the upper air that helped the thunderstorms build initially is much colder than the surface air, it isn't long before the rising, warmer air heats up the air aloft and it begins to flow away from the top of the storm. This provides an exhaust port for the developing system, lowering the pressure at the surface even more and causing large quantities of humid air to be drawn into the rotating cyclone.

Feeding Frenzy

As the storm spins up, a chain reaction begins: more outflow at the top lets more hot air in at the bottom, resulting in faster surface winds pouring in and spiraling up through the storm's center. Until the winds reach 39 miles per hour, the storm is known as a tropical depression, and its main threat is rain and the potential for flooding if it moves over mountainous terrain or stalls over any landmass for an extended period.

When wind speeds exceed 39 miles per hour, the system is called a tropical storm and the National Hurricane Center assigns it a name from a list established by the WMO (World Meteorological Organization). The Atlantic Basin is assigned six lists of names, with one list being used each year. After six years, the first list is used again. If an especially destructive hurricane develops, its name is retired and no future storm will ever bear that name.

A 'CANE IS BORN

A tropical cyclone is known as a tropical storm until its winds reach 73 miles per hour, when it officially becomes a hurricane. At that point, it can be measured on the Saffir-Simpson Hurricane Wind Scale, a method of rating hurricanes developed by Herbert Saffir, an engineer who became interested in how wind causes damage to buildings, and Robert Simpson, who was director of the National Hurricane Center in the 1970s. The scale rates hurricanes by their wind speed, barometric pressure, storm surge height, and damage potential in categories from 1 to 5. After Hurricane Floyd in 1999, which caused extensive flooding in eastern North Carolina, a need for an additional scale that would measure the risk of flooding was identified; its creation is still a work in progress.

Hypercanes

Although no recent hurricane has exceeded Category 5, MIT researchers theorize prehistoric hurricanes may have reached 750 miles per hour or more. These "hypercanes" could have formed after asteroid impacts, and might have wiped out whole species.

In the meantime, the categories and their characteristics break down as follows:

Category 1

Wind speeds of 73 to 95 miles per hour. Category 1 storms are the least destructive hurricanes where winds are concerned. Most damage is usually confined to trees, shrubs, and unanchored mobile homes, although flooding can cause much more harm than wind. As the hurricane grows, it forms an eye in the center, a circle of relative calm where the sky may be blue and the winds light. Surrounding this area is an eye wall, a ring of intense thunderstorms that spin around the center of the hurricane.

Category 2

Winds of 96 to 110 miles per hour. The storm surge, a giant dome of water that moves along with the hurricane, can be from 6 to 8 feet above normal, causing coastal areas to flood in advance of the storm. Doors, windows, and roofing materials are all at risk in a Category 2 hurricane.

Category 3

Winds range from 111 to 130 miles per hour. This storm kicks it up another notch, flooding low-lying areas near the coast with a storm surge 9 to 12 feet above sea level. The surge can move inland up to 8 miles, requiring some evacuations. At these wind speeds, mobile homes are completely destroyed and even concrete block homes sustain some damage. The foliage of shrubs and trees is blown off, and many trees are uprooted by the wind. Large structures near the beach are battered by floating debris carried by high waves.

Category 4

Winds of 131 to 155 miles per hour. Once a hurricane has this strength, you know it's extremely dangerous. Low-lying areas may be flooded hours before the storm moves ashore, and mass evacuations are necessary. The storm surge can reach a towering 13 to 18 feet above normal, causing major damage to any structures near the shore. The roofs are stripped off some homes and other buildings, and even external walls may fail. Signs, trees, and shrubs are torn from the ground and become flying missiles.

Category 5

Winds are *sustained* at over 155 miles per hour. Fortunately, Category 5 storms are rare, but they are among the most treacherous winds on Earth. With a storm surge of more than 18 feet, these hurricanes leave major devastation in their wake. There is extensive damage to even strong buildings, and the complete destruction of others, especially those near the shoreline. Category 4 and 5 hurricanes making landfall near inhabited areas have caused some of the worst damage and loss of life in our nation's history. One such storm was Hugo, a giant storm that brought the highest storm surge ever recorded on the east coast of the United States—nearly 20 feet above sea level.

STORM SURGE: A HURRICANE'S MOST DEADLY WEAPON

NOAA estimates that nine out of every ten victims of hurricanes are killed by storm surge. Because hurricanes are huge low-pressure systems, some think the surge is caused by the storm's lower atmospheric pressure raising the sea level. While that effect is real and measurable, it is so small as to be insignificant when a hurricane makes landfall.

The storm surge is caused by the hurricane's winds piling water up ahead of the eye as it moves toward shore. As long as the hurricane is in the open ocean, there is no storm surge to speak of, because water that gets pushed up ahead of the storm has room to flow away. But as the storm approaches the coast, there is no room for the water to escape and it rapidly rises, sometimes in a matter of minutes, into a mountain of water. How high the storm surge will be above average sea level and how much damage it will do depends on several factors. One is wind speed: a Category 4 storm will have a higher storm surge and cause much more destruction than a Category 2, for instance.

The Storm Surge

The storm surge isn't just another wave pushed ahead of a storm; it acts like a gigantic bulldozer that can destroy anything in its path. Think of the storm surge as a moving wall of water weighing millions of tons.

But just as important as the hurricane's wind speed is where you are in respect to the hurricane's eye. If you're behind and above a hurricane looking toward its direction of motion, the front part on the right side will have the highest wind speeds. That's because the hurricane's forward speed is added to the wind speed in that area, called the right front quadrant (RFQ). So, if a hurricane approaching land has sustained winds of 100 miles per hour, and it's moving forward at a speed of 20 miles per hour (a fairly fast-moving hurricane, by the way), winds in the RFQ will be measured by a stationary ground observer at 120 miles per hour. As you might guess, winds on the left side of a hurricane are rotating in the opposite direction, and won't cause as much damage.

Direction Makes a Difference

The storm's angle of attack is a key factor in its impact. The highest level of destruction is caused by a hurricane hitting the coastline head-on, just as in an automobile accident. If a storm travels up the coast, with its left side brushing the seashore, the most dangerous part of the storm stays offshore and the net effect will be much less damage.

Shoreline and Ocean Bottom

The shapes of the shoreline and the ocean bottom have a great deal to do with the magnitude of a storm surge. The worst damage occurs when a developing surge meets a shallow seabed sloping gently to the beach. This is why areas like New Orleans are especially at risk.

The worst-case scenario would be a hurricane arriving onshore at high tide. With the ocean level already at its highest point of the day, the storm surge from a Category 4 or 5 hurricane can add another 15 or 20 feet of water, with abnormally large waves breaking on top of that. Water weighs around 1,700 pounds per cubic yard, and there are few structures that can stand up to the abuse a high storm surge can produce.

TORNADOES

Terrifying Twisters

Packing the fastest winds on Earth, F5 tornadoes are truly terrifying apparitions. But even smaller tornadoes can wreak unbelievable destruction. Incredibly, some people spend significant amounts of money and time trying to get closer to them.

A CHASER'S VIEW

On May 30, 1998, storm chasers Martin Lisius and Keith Brown were following a supercell across the rolling hills of South Dakota when they came over a ridge and saw a rapidly moving tornado to the west. With lightning crashing around them, the two men stopped and captured several still pictures and some movies of the twister, which was now nearly a mile wide at its base. As the vortex entered an area of trees, they saw bright flashes of light as power lines and transformers arced and exploded. They didn't realize it at the time, but they were witnessing the destruction of the town of Spencer.

At the end of the day the chasers convened at a restaurant in Sioux Falls, exuberant after their successful hunt. As they compared notes on the day's events, a television in the restaurant broadcast a bulletin about the storm. The group grew silent as the news unfolded: the tornado had killed six people, injured more than one-third of the town's 320 residents, and destroyed most of its 190 buildings.

WE'RE NUMBER ONE!

The United States has the dubious distinction of being the tornado capital of the world, averaging more than 800 of the killer storms each year. In 1992 a record 1,293 tornadoes formed in America. Although tornadoes have been recorded in every state in the Union, most occur in the Tornado Alley states of Oklahoma, Texas, Nebraska, and Kansas, as well as in many southern states. Unlike hurricanes, which satellites can spot in their formative stages over a period of days, tornadoes form too quickly to study over a long period. This makes tornadoes an extremely dangerous short-term threat.

Dust Devils

The gentlest type of whirlwind is the dust devil, caused by the Sun heating up the ground at different rates. Air rising faster in one area than in another nearby causes a weak low-pressure system to form. The air in adjacent areas flows into it, creating a spinning parcel of air that picks up dust, dirt, or leaves in its path.

Also unlike hurricanes, which may last for a week or more, most tornadoes last only a few minutes, and their paths average a mere 4 miles in length. They generally move along the ground at 20 to 50 miles per hour, but a few have been clocked doing more than 70. They're a lot smaller than hurricanes, too, usually only 400 to 500 feet wide, although some monster storms grow to a girth of more than a mile. Tornadoes almost always turn in a counterclockwise direction in the Northern Hemisphere and clockwise in the Southern

Hemisphere. A very few twisters somehow overcome the Coriolis force and rotate in the opposite direction of the norm.

Killer Winds

Tornadoes may be smaller than hurricanes, but what they lack in size they make up for in intensity. While a Category 5 hurricane, the strongest on Earth, has winds of more than 155 miles per hour, the winds of some tornadoes exceed speeds of 300 miles per hour. Add to that the fact that these awe-inspiring funnels can descend from the clouds at a moment's notice, and you have one very dangerous weather phenomenon on your hands.

In 1949, Edward M. Brooks of St. Louis University was examining the data from weather stations situated near the paths of tornadoes when he discovered a link between twisters and mesocyclones, the large rotating air masses found in supercells. In 1953 the first mesocyclone was actually seen on radar at Urbana, Illinois. It appeared as a hook shape, since the radar beam was reflecting off rain that was being drawn into a rotating cylinder of air within the storm. These classic "hook echoes" are still looked for on modern radar screens as evidence of possible tornado formation.

STORM CHASERS

The man who really put tornadoes on the map was Dr. Tetsuya "Ted" Fujita, who developed a scale of tornado intensity measurement that's still in use today. Fujita became interested in weather in his native Japan and came to the United States in 1953 to further his research in mesoscale meteorology.

Soon Fujita became interested in the damage caused by tornadoes and began collecting aerial photos of twister debris, hoping to find patterns that would help him understand the internal structure of tornadoes. In one image he noted "cycloidal marks," or smaller swirls of damage within the larger path of a tornado that had torn through a cornfield. Fujita deduced that they had come from minitornadoes spinning around the vortex of the main twister. Later observations proved him right.

After years of studying piles of debris and other damage left behind by twisters, in 1971 Fujita (now known as "Mr. Tornado") developed his famous Fujita Scale, or F-scale. The Fujita Scale was based on the damage a tornado would do to "strong frame houses," and although the scientific community took him to task because there was no direct verification of his conclusions, his scale has proved remarkably accurate.

Microbursts

After an Eastern Airlines crash in 1975, Fujita examined the flight records of other planes in the area and discovered that some had experienced updrafts while others fought severe downdrafts. His research led him to postulate the existence of microbursts, violent but compact columns of air rushing toward the ground that could cause planes to crash on landing or takeoff.

Ted Fujita died on November 19, 1998, at the age of seventy-eight, leaving one of the most remarkable legacies in meteorology. He was not always right in every assumption and theory, but unlike many scientists, he never feared being wrong. "Even if I am wrong 50 percent of the time," he once said, "that would still be a tremendous contribution to meteorology." And so it was.

THE FUJITA SCALE		
F#	**DAMAGE**	**WIND SPEED**
F0	Light	Up to 72 mph
F1	Moderate	73 to 112 mph
F2	Considerable	113 to 157 mph
F3	Severe	158 to 206 mph
F4	Devastating	207 to 260 mph
F5	Incredible	Above 261 mph

TORNADO FORMATION

Recipe for a Twister

Meteorologists know which conditions may spawn a tornado, but the actual birth process within a thunderstorm is still up for debate. The most likely scenario: a warm, humid layer of air forms near the ground under a layer of colder air in the upper atmosphere. When you have warm air near cooler air, you get an unstable atmosphere, and when there's wind shear between the layers, a rotation forms.

If a layer of hot, dry air becomes established between the warm, humid air below and the cooler air aloft, it forms a boundary called a "convective cap" that keeps the layer near the surface from rising. A convective cap acts like the radiator cap on your car, keeping the atmosphere from boiling over. As solar energy passes through the cap, it heats up the humid air at ground level, which pressurizes the cap like steam in a radiator.

More Tornado Formation

Tornadoes can form in other ways too: they often spring up within hurricanes, which already contain all the heat, rotation, and moisture that a tornado needs for survival. Tornadoes can even form in the winter during intense storms. Winter tornadoes are most common near the Gulf of Mexico, when warmer air collides with advancing storm systems.

Now add a dryline, or cold front, into the scenario: the convective cap can weaken to the point where all that built-up warmth near the surface explodes through the layer of hot air, mixing with the colder air above it to form a supercell, with strong updrafts rotating rapidly upward through the cloud. As the thunderstorm builds higher, a rotating "wall cloud" descends beneath the storm—the direct precursor to a tornado. Some theorists say that a tube of air spinning horizontally near the surface (like a rolling pin) can get picked up by the updrafts at this point, and with the tube now spinning vertically, a funnel cloud forms. Within the funnel is a strong downdraft, which descends toward the ground, creating a tornado.

Gustnadoes and Landspouts

Sometimes small whirlpools of wind form on the leading edges of gust fronts and are called gustnadoes. They're not really tornadoes since they're not connected to the cloud base, but they can still cause damage. On June 9, 1994, a line of strong thunderstorms racing through central Tennessee spawned a gustnado that passed within 100 yards of the Memphis National Weather Service, causing F1-level damage to houses and apartments nearby. Some gustnadoes have been clocked at speeds of up to 110 miles per hour.

Another type of tornado that doesn't form in a supercell is the landspout, a weak column of spinning winds. These usually occur in Colorado and Florida. Unlike their larger cousins, landspouts don't generally show up on Doppler radar and their life cycles are much shorter than a tornado's. Landspouts usually form beneath building cumulus clouds, and although relatively weak, a few become powerful enough to cause serious damage.

Whirling Water

A landspout over water is called—wait for it—a waterspout, and is also one of the weaker types of atmospheric funnels. In this case the word *weaker* is relative: a few of these seagoing cyclones can spin at speeds of up to 190 miles per hour, but they never reach the 300-miles-per-hour-plus velocity of an F5 tornado. Waterspouts form when moist humid air is pulled into a rotating updraft over a body of water. Until the rotation reaches a speed of 40 miles per hour or so, the funnel may be invisible. But as moisture begins to condense, a column of spinning water vapor reaches down from the cloud toward the surface. Waterspouts look like they're sucking huge amounts of water into the clouds, but it's really just vapor. Sometimes waterspouts can move inland and become tornadoes.

SEEING IT COMING

In the last few years, millions of dollars and thousands of hours have been spent learning how to predict these storms using sophisticated Doppler radar and other electronic methods. But the very first tornado forecast was accomplished back in 1948 without the aid of today's high-tech gadgetry.

On March 20, California native Robert C. Miller, an Air Force captain and meteorologist, was putting together the evening forecast for Tinker Air Force Base in Oklahoma where he was stationed. Miller and Ernest Fawbush, a fellow forecaster, analyzed the latest weather maps from Washington and concluded it would be a relatively quiet night, with moderately strong winds but no storms, and that's what their 9 p.m. forecast predicted. The two men didn't realize that some of their source data were erroneous until a strong twister tore through the base an hour later, narrowly missing the aircraft hangars and operations center, and blowing the windows out of nearly every building on the base.

A Second Chance

Five days later, on March 25, Miller was producing the morning charts when he noticed that the day's expected weather conditions would be almost identical to those on the day of the tornado. He alerted General Fred S. Borum, who was by now in charge of the operation. The general ordered Miller to issue a thunderstorm warning, and by 2 p.m. a squall line had formed, just as it had before the last tornado.

"Are you going to issue a tornado forecast?" the general asked. Miller and Fawbush hemmed and hawed, neither relishing the idea of having another blown forecast pinned on them. "We both made abortive efforts at crawling out of such a horrendous decision," said Miller in his memoirs. "We pointed out the infinitesimal possibility of a second tornado striking the same area within twenty years or more, let alone in five days. 'Besides,' we said, 'no one has ever issued an operational tornado forecast.'"

"You are about to set a precedent," said the general.

On the Money

The forecast was composed, typed, and sent to Base Operations. A weather alert was sounded and base personnel flew into action, securing planes in hangars and tying down loose objects. At 5 p.m. a squall line passed through a nearby airport, but with only light rain and some small hail. Dejected, Miller drove home to commiserate with his wife. Later that evening as the couple was listening to the radio, an announcer broke in with an urgent bulletin about a tornado at Tinker Field.

Miller rushed back to the base to find a scene of devastation, with power poles down and debris strewn everywhere. Miller relates what a jubilant Major Fawbush told him he'd missed:

"As the line approached the southwest corner of the field, two thunderstorms seemed to join and quickly took on a greenish black hue. They could observe a slow counterclockwise cloud rotation around the point at which the storms merged. Suddenly a large cone shaped cloud bulged down rotating counterclockwise at great speed. At the same time they saw a wing from one of the moth-balled World War II B-29s float lazily upward toward the visible part of the funnel. A second or two later the wing disintegrated, the funnel shot to the ground and the second large tornado in five days began its devastating journey across the base very close to the track of its predecessor."

Warning Centers

Buoyed by their success, the Air Force set up the National Severe Storms Forecast Center, now the National Weather Service's Storm Prediction Center, in 1951, and soon the public was clamoring for its own storm warnings. In 1952 the Weather Bureau finally set up its own storm prediction agency, the Weather Bureau Severe Weather Unit, which became the Storm Prediction Center in 1995.

Introducing Doppler

In 1971, the same year Ted Fujita came up with his tornado damage scale, Doppler radar was first used to confirm that winds within a hook echo were rotating, giving scientists a picture of a storm's internal mesocyclone—the "smoking gun" that pointed to the origins of tornadoes. In 1973, Doppler radar pinpointed an area in a thunderstorm near Union City, Oklahoma, where winds abruptly changed direction, which turned out to coincide with the occurrence of a violent tornado. For the first time meteorologists had direct evidence that Doppler radar could spot a twister in its formative stages.

A CLOSER LOOK

Doppler is great if a tornado happens to pass by a radar installation, but few twisters are that accommodating. In 1994 and 1995, NOAA's National Severe Storms Laboratory (NSSL) formed a plan to hunt tornadoes on their own turf, taking the war to the enemy for the first time. The main purpose of the VORTEX1 project (Verification of the Origins of Rotation in Tornadoes Experiment 1) was to find out exactly how and under what conditions tornadoes form.

After formulating twenty-two hypotheses for the project to either prove or disprove, Dr. Erik Rasmussen was assigned the role of project director and field coordinator, and several universities were brought on board to aid in the project and analyze the data. Unlike previous efforts to study tornadoes, all the equipment and manpower available would be brought to bear on only one storm at a time, analyzing each twister in exhaustive detail to obtain as much data as possible from different vantage points and with myriad instrument types.

Twelve cars and five vans were outfitted with the latest in sensors designed to measure temperature, humidity, wind speed, and air pressure. The data would be gathered every six seconds and stored for later analysis and comparison. Another van would serve as a traveling command post where the field commander could constantly monitor the position of the other vehicles. The vans were equipped with weather balloons designed to transmit upper-air information back to the convoy, which would form a "mobile mesonet" (a network of weather and environmental monitoring stations) that could cover the tornado from all angles.

A Phalanx of Sensors

The crown jewel of project VORTEX1 was a mobile Doppler radar unit mounted on a truck that would allow researchers to intercept and study supercells and tornadoes wherever they occurred. This "Doppler on wheels" would become the most important element during the hunt, peering deep inside a supercell's mesocyclone to watch the actual birth of a twister.

Orbiting overhead as the convoy spread out around a storm were NOAA's WP-3D Orion (the same type of aircraft used by the famed Hurricane Hunters of the 53rd Weather Reconnaissance Squadron of the Air Force Reserve) and a Lockheed Electra owned by NCAR. The two planes gave the project three-dimensional coverage of any target, using their belly radars to scan horizontally to determine a storm's internal structure, and their tail radar to scan vertically for wind speed information.

VORTEX1 launched in 1994. That year turned out to be one of the slowest ever for tornadoes in the target area. Even though there were no twisters to study, scientists practiced deploying the mobile mesonet and were able to gather data on several supercell thunderstorms.

A Major Success

Things changed in 1995, when the team was able to intercept nine tornadoes and study them at close range. One tornado that formed near Dimmitt, Texas, became the most intensely examined twister in history. On June 2, after gathering data on a tornado that destroyed part of the town of Friona, Texas, radar showed another mesocyclone forming near Dimmitt. The teams quickly moved into their assigned positions around the developing storm, and just as quickly a tornado formed south of the town. The team was able to capture high-resolution Doppler data of the debris cloud caused by the tornado, as well as some video footage.

The tornado evolved into a powerful F4, literally sucking the pavement off a stretch of State Highway 86 and snapping telephone poles like matchsticks. Several vehicles were destroyed, and two trucks disappeared completely. Ten miles away, another tornado had formed, so the Electra was able to gather data from only one side of the Dimmitt storm. Even so, the planes were able to document how air flowed through the mesocyclone. Ground units meanwhile collected nearly 1,000 automated surface observations near the storm and around 1,000 additional measurements by balloon and other methods.

Some of the findings include:

- Most of the elements that lead to tornadoes are present in one small part of a supercell, allowing scientists to narrow their focus.
- Tornadoes can form rapidly at the beginning of a storm's life, in less than half an hour from the formation of the supercell.
- Before a tornado forms, a large invisible rotating segment of the storm's mesocylone already extends to ground level.

In 1997 a follow-up to the project, called Sub-VORTEX, was conducted, but with fewer vehicles and a tighter focus. Sub-VORTEX used two Doppler radar trucks to look into the same tornado from different angles, forming a two-dimensional image of the storm's interior.

In 2009 another project was launched under the name VORTEX2 to study why some thunderstorms produce tornadoes, while others don't. Although many questions remain, the VORTEX projects have substantially increased our knowledge of this dangerous weather phenomenon.

VOLCANOES AND OTHER DISASTERS

Impacting the Weather

The pristine, snow-covered summit of Mount St. Helens in Washington State had been living up to its American Indian name *Louwala-Clough*, or "smoking mountain," for two months when dawn broke on May 18, 1980. The volcano that some called "America's Mount Fuji" had been rumbling and emitting steam for so long that many nearby residents had nearly stopped hearing it. But at 8:32 that morning, a magnitude 5.1 earthquake centered a mile beneath the mountain caused its entire north flank to collapse.

A huge avalanche of melting ice, earth, and debris raced downslope at speeds of up to 180 miles per hour. And without the burden of its outer shell, gas and steam that had built up to tremendous pressure within the mountain caused it to literally explode in a lateral blast that was heard hundreds of miles away.

Moving horizontally at nearly 670 miles per hour, just below the speed of sound, a hellish wall of magma, ash, and volcanic debris destroyed everything in its path to a distance of 19 miles from the mountain.

Following the lateral explosion, a plume of ash and steam launched skyward, reaching an altitude of 12 miles in ten minutes, finally punching through the stratosphere where it began to spread out. Around the remains of the mountain, lightning forked through the thick, swirling ash, starting forest fires. By noon, the cities of Yakima and Spokane were covered in a thick blanket of gray, choking ash. Before it was over, fifty-seven people were dead.

Scenes of the eruption of Mount St. Helens burned themselves into the national consciousness, and the explosion was the largest in the recorded history of the United States. But there have been far larger explosions, and their effect on the atmosphere has been much greater.

THE BIG BLASTS

Television crews usually focus on spectacular fountains and streams of lava when covering erupting volcanoes, and no one will argue that they don't make compelling subjects. Volcanoes can eject lava bombs—blobs of magma the size of coconuts or larger—which are just as hazardous as they sound, and produce pyroclastic flows, which are avalanches of superheated gases, hot ash, pumice, and melted rock that can race down a mountainside at 100 miles per hour. But those effects are confined to a small area around the eruption. Far greater and more widespread are the effects of ash and other particles flung into the stratosphere by these exploding mountains.

Mount St. Helens and the Climate

Once dust and ash are injected into the upper atmosphere by a volcanic eruption, the debris can remain suspended there for years. Fortunately, the eruption of Mount St. Helens had no significant effect on global climate, due largely to the fact that most of its force was directed sideways instead of upward.

During the twentieth century two volcanoes had a huge impact on Earth's climate: El Chichon in Mexico and Mount Pinatubo in the

Philippines. The Mexican volcano spewed 120 tons of material in 1982 into the atmosphere, and Pinatubo disgorged a stunning 310 tons in 1991, laden with caustic chemicals such as sulfur dioxide and hydrogen chloride, which can damage Earth's ozone layer.

As sulfur particles from volcanic eruptions drift in the upper atmosphere, they combine with water vapor, and as the particles are bombarded with sunlight, they mutate into sulfuric acid, which forms a hazy layer that reflects solar radiation back into space. With less solar energy reaching the surface, temperatures begin to drop. After the eruption of Mount Pinatubo, average global temperatures fell 1.5°F.

Volcanic Threats

The Cascade Range of the Pacific Northwest is home to more than a dozen potentially active volcanoes, including Mount St. Helens, and most of them tend to erupt explosively. The US Geological Survey has set up a Volcano Hazards Program to watch these potential trouble spots, since some, like Mount Hood and Mount Rainier, are close to major cities.

A link between volcanic eruptions and global climate change was first established after the eruption of Krakatau, in the Sunda Strait between Java and Sumatra. The volcano, also known as Krakatoa, exploded in 1883 with a blast said to have been the loudest sound ever heard on Earth. Ten times more powerful than Mount St. Helens, the eruption instantly vaporized two-thirds of the volcano and caused tsunamis—giant waves more than 100 hundred feet high—that killed more than 36,000 people. Its dust cloud covered two million square miles, lowering global temperatures for five years. The blast set off seismometers all over the world, and for the first time, scientists were able to gather observations from widely spaced locations in order to study the explosion.

Krakatau Sunsets

Accounts of Krakatau's aftermath include tales of brilliant sunsets that could be seen all over the world for weeks after the eruption, caused by the enormous quantity of ash pumped into the stratosphere by the blast. The sky became so bright in New York and Connecticut that some residents thought their cities were ablaze and called local fire departments.

THE MOTHER OF ALL ERUPTIONS

Even Krakatau wasn't the largest volcanic eruption in recorded history: sixty-eight years earlier, a volcano named Tambora exploded in Indonesia, spewing 150 times more ash into the upper atmosphere than Mount St. Helens did in 1980. The column of dust, ash, and debris rose to a height of 28 miles before collapsing on itself, causing devastating pyroclastic flows to sweep down to the ocean. Around 10,000 people died in the explosion and its immediate aftermath, but Tambora wasn't through causing misery.

In the months to come, thousands more would die on nearby islands as epidemics and famine swept through their midst. As the unimaginably huge cloud of ash spread farther across the globe, it began to trigger climate changes far and wide. In China the skies above Hainan Island went black, obliterating the Sun and destroying crops and trees.

Frankenstein

On the shores of Lake Geneva, Switzerland, in 1816, the gloomy weather prompted Lord Byron to suggest that his houseguests join him in a ghost story–writing contest. Byron and Percy Shelley abandoned their attempts before long, but Shelley's wife, Mary, conjured a story of a scientist named Frankenstein that made literary history.

By the next year, known as "the year without a summer," economic losses were piling up as far away as North America. In June 1816, severe frosts killed Northeast farmers' crops as they repeatedly tried to replant. In Vermont foot-long icicles hung from the trees while ice an inch thick covered ponds and lakes. Newly shorn sheep died by the thousands, and so did migratory birds caught in the icy weather's grip. At Williamstown, Vermont, the temperature at 5 p.m. one June day was recorded at 30.5°F.

Things weren't much better in Europe, which was just recuperating from the Napoleonic Wars. In Britain and France riots broke out as food shortages loomed, and in Switzerland the violence caused the government to declare a state of national emergency.

FORECAST: EXPLOSIVE

After studying eruptions for decades, volcanologists now understand that a volcano's history is one major key in forecasting its future. Volcanoes such as Kilauea in Hawaii erupt on a regular basis and in a predictable manner, and because they don't generally erupt explosively, they can be monitored with sensitive instruments that provide clues to the conditions that exist just before an eruption.

Seismicity

Volcanoes give many clues before erupting, including underground earthquakes that become more frequent and intense before a blast—activity that scientists call seismicity. Volcanologists can now measure and track the shock waves generated by these temblors with seismometers, which record quakes' magnitude and epicenters as magma flows deep below the surface.

Angle of Attack

Melted rock can also push upward toward the surface until the volcano's "skin" is distorted into a pressure-filled dome. Before Mount St. Helens erupted in 1980, the mountain began to develop a huge bulge on its north face that grew at the rate of more than 5 feet per day. Geologists were able to track the growth of the bulge using a device called a geodimeter, which can measure very small changes in distance with reflected light. By the day of the eruption, the instruments showed that some parts of the north face had bulged outward more than 450 feet from their original positions.

Predicting Volcanoes

Scientists are getting some assistance from space in their continuing quest to accurately predict volcanic outbursts. Earth-observing satellites can spot rising underground pools of magma from orbit. The upwellings, which often precede an eruption, show up as "hot spots" on digital images.

Scientists also employed tiltmeters at St. Helens. As their name implies, these devices can measure minute changes in the slope angle or tilt of the ground. Tiltmeters work much like a carpenter's level: the movement of a bubble floating in conducting fluid is monitored electronically, and any change in the bubble's position is translated into a degree of tilt and relayed to a base station. Tiltmeters are so sensitive they can measure a change in angle as small as 0.00006 of a degree!

Another tool used in forecasting eruptions is a correlation spectrometer, which measures how much sulfur dioxide is being emitted by a volcano. These emissions tend to increase markedly before an eruption.

Positive Predictions

In 1991 scientists were able to use all these devices to successfully predict the eruption of Mount Pinatubo. It first gave warning by generating a series of earthquakes, followed by an increase in sulfur dioxide emissions. Then, the sides of the volcano began to swell outward. Alarmed authorities evacuated nearby Clark Air Base and 58,000 residents who lived within 20 miles of the volcano just days before the mountain exploded in one of the most powerful eruptions of the twentieth century.

THE JOHNSTOWN FLOOD

Rising Waters

When the South Fork Fishing and Hunting Club bought 400-acre Lake Conemaugh and seventy acres of land near Johnstown, Pennsylvania, in 1879, the aim was to provide a fishing and vacation retreat for wealthy Pittsburgh industrialists and businessmen such as Andrew Carnegie, Henry Frick, and Andrew Mellon.

The earthen dam that held back the lake's waters had fallen into disrepair, so the club's president, Benjamin Ruff, began reinforcing it with rocks, hay, mud, and tree stumps, and didn't bother to replace the discharge pipes that had been removed by the previous owner. Although plagued by problems, the construction was finally finished in 1881, leaving the new dam 72 feet high and 918 feet wide. The lake was stocked with black bass and the clubhouse was opened soon afterward.

Johnstown lay 14 miles downstream in a floodplain at the fork of the Little Conemaugh and Stonycreek Rivers. Many of the town's 30,000 residents viewed the dam as a menace; no engineer had planned its reconstruction, and the 3-mile-long lake loomed a full 450 feet above the town. Said one worried resident, "No one could see the immense height to which that artificial dam had been built without fearing the tremendous power of the water behind it. . . . People asked why the dam was not strengthened, as it certainly had become weak, but nothing was done, and by and by they talked less and less about it."

BUILDUP TO DISASTER

On May 30, 1889, a hard rain began and continued through the night. The US Signal Service estimated that 6–8 inches of rain fell in just twenty-four hours, carrying 10,000 cubic feet of water into Lake Conemaugh each minute—enough to fill an Olympic-sized swimming pool every three and a half minutes. By morning, the club's resident engineer, John Parke Jr., saw that the water level was only 4 feet below the top of the dam, its twenty million gallons putting immense pressure on the earthworks. Repeated attempts to shore up the weakened structure failed, and at 11:30 a.m., Parke jumped on his horse and galloped down to the town of South Fork directly below the dam to warn of the danger. He also sent two men to the South Fork telegraph station to alert Johnstown.

Because Johnstown was located in a floodplain, periodic inundations were nothing new to the residents, and many ignored the warnings. At ten minutes after 3 p.m. on May 31, the dam collapsed, and a wall of water 40 feet high swept down the narrow valley, tearing out trees, boulders, and telegraph poles and adding them to its boiling fury. The inhabitants of Johnstown heard a low rumble in the distance that soon turned into "a roar like thunder," as one survivor would later describe it.

First came a violent wind that blew down frame houses, and then the 40-foot wave crashed into the town, pulverizing buildings with huge chunks of debris carried by the raging waters. When the flood smashed through a wire factory, miles of barbed wire were added to the thundering debris. The deluge swept onward, racing through the town until its thousands of tons of wreckage encountered the old stone railroad bridge below the river's fork.

THE BRIDGE TO HELL

Forty-five acres of timber, rock, and barbed wire smashed many victims against the bridge, and some of those who escaped being crushed were burned to death as the oily mass caught fire. As rescue workers desperately attempted to reach the victims, some of whom were still trapped in the remains of their homes, the flames spread until they engulfed the entire mass of debris, burning with "all the fury of hell" according to one newspaper account. In all, 2,209 people lost their lives in the flood.

An Act of God

Although the South Fork Fishing and Hunting Club was clearly to blame for the disaster, lawsuits filed after the flood were dismissed, since judges considered the incident to be an act of God. The American Red Cross, which had been formed only seven years earlier, arrived in Johnstown on June 5, and Red Cross founder Clara Barton was among the relief workers.

It took Johnstown five years to recover from the disaster, and yet no legislation was enacted to protect residents from future floods. In fact, despite the considerable loss of life, it would take more deaths and forty-seven more years before serious flood control efforts were begun.

THE GREAT GALVESTON HURRICANE

A City at Risk

Even today when we have early warning systems in place to alert us to coming weather dangers, hurricanes can be devastating in their impact. At the beginning of the twentieth century, when those systems did not exist, a massive hurricane was apocalyptic.

THE GREAT GALVESTON HURRICANE

As the residents of Galveston, Texas, opened their morning papers on Saturday, September 8, 1900, many noticed a small news item on page 3 about a tropical storm in the Gulf of Mexico. Due to the lack of effective communication channels, no further information was available. But the Weather Bureau had issued a storm warning the previous day, and sure enough, clouds and gusty winds were blowing over the city as many residents left home to put in the last day of what was for most a typical six-day workweek.

Known by many as the "New York of the South," Galveston in 1900 was a prosperous city of 38,000 people looking forward to the new century. Home of the only deepwater port on the Texas coast, it was also the thriving center of America's cotton export business; the kind of place where millions of dollars could be made by those with the right connections. In short, it was a great place to live.

But the city had an Achilles' heel: it was built on an island of sand some 30 miles long, separated from the mainland by 2-mile-wide

Galveston Bay. The island's average height above sea level was only 4.5 feet in 1900, but residents had been assured by meteorologists and geographers alike that the wide, sloping sea bottom that led to the island protected them against incoming storms.

One such meteorologist was local Weather Bureau chief Isaac M. Cline, who had long maintained that the island was not only safe from hurricanes, but that anyone who felt differently was delusional. So far, Cline had been right: major storms had hit Galveston in the past, but none of them had caused severe damage, and as residents left their homes for work, they were secure in the belief that their city was safe.

A Theory Disproved

But Cline was startled to see the barometer plummeting that Saturday morning, the tide rising steadily against a strong offshore wind that should have kept it at bay. Cline took to his horse-drawn carriage and raced down to the beach, telling everyone he encountered to get to higher ground. Few listened: the waves crashing on the beach were a magnificent spectacle, and many had traveled from the mainland just to see them.

But as the storm approached land, the wind shifted, and with nothing to hold them back, the Gulf waters crashed into beachside homes and other buildings, shattering them to bits. Terrified residents ran inland, but there was nowhere to go: the bridges to the mainland had been destroyed by an errant barge, and rising waters were intruding from Galveston Bay, trapping thousands.

By 3 p.m. the entire island was submerged, and refugees climbed onto roofs and into trees to escape the steadily rising water. At 5:15 the Weather Service anemometer blew away after recording gusts of 100 miles per hour, and at 6:30 a giant storm wave driven ashore by the approaching eye of the hurricane suddenly raised the water level to 15 feet. As the waves crashed through the darkening city, they tore entire buildings from their foundations and swept them into the bay.

Some who tried to make their way to safer shelters at the height of the storm were killed by slate shingles flung from rooftops, while others were bombarded with flying bricks and timber. As floodwaters rose around St. Mary's Orphanage, nuns frantically rushed their young charges to the newly built girls' dormitory. But by nightfall, the winds were screaming at an estimated 150 miles an hour, and after the dormitory's roof collapsed, the nuns cut down a clothesline and lashed it around the children like mountain climbers to keep everyone together. Sadly, the orphanage collapsed in the midst of the gale, sweeping ninety-three children and ten nuns into the black, churning water.

A Staggering Death Toll

The next morning, stunned survivors were met with a scene of utter desolation. Many of those who had ridden out the storm were naked, having been stripped of their clothing by wind and water-driven debris. Galveston Bay was adrift with dead bodies, both human and animal, and as many as 30,000 people were left homeless. The number of deaths was estimated to be between 8,000 and 12,000, but the poor recordkeeping of the time made it impossible to be sure.

Isaac Cline survived, but sadly, his pregnant wife did not; her body was later found in a mound of debris. Three boys from St. Mary's Orphanage were found clinging to a tree, bruised and battered but still alive, the only orphan survivors of that fateful night. Many families had been completely wiped out by the storm, which became known as the deadliest natural disaster in the history of the United States.

With rising heat and humidity, disposal of the thousands of bodies became a priority. At first, barges were loaded with bodies and sunk in the Gulf, but when the corpses began washing up on the beaches, burning became the preferred method. By the following Tuesday, funeral pyres were burning all over the city. The grisly job of stacking and incinerating the bodies fell to laborers, who were plied with whiskey to dull their senses; others were forced to perform the thankless task at gunpoint.

Reconstruction and Remembrance

Clara Barton arrived to care for the survivors of the hurricane in what would be her last relief mission. The Red Cross founder was now seventy-eight years old, but she was still able to establish an orphanage and help obtain lumber for the rebuilding process, raising money by selling photographs of the devastation. Barton later wrote of the scene, describing it as being so horrific that her workers "grew pale and ill" and that even she, who had seen so much heartbreak and devastation in her life, "needed the help of a steadying hand as I walked to the waiting Pullman on the track, courteously tendered free of charge to take us away."

With Galveston's sense of security literally gone with the wind, efforts were begun to construct a 17-foot-high seawall that would run 3 miles along the shoreline. In addition, the entire city was raised as high as 17 feet by propping buildings up on pilings and pumping fill underneath. In 1915 another hurricane struck Galveston, but only eight people died, proving that the city's efforts to protect itself had been successful.

Galveston is no stranger to big storms. Hurricane Rita hit the area in 2005, and Texas officials ordered a mass evacuation. Unfortunately, many roads were clogged, and in the heat as many as 118 deaths were reported. More big storms can be expected in the future. So despite the seawall and other precautions, Galveston remains a city at risk.

THE SUPER OUTBREAK

A Perfect Storm

On April 2, 1974, a cold air mass over the Rocky Mountains was heading directly toward a warmer blanket of humid air flowing northward from the Gulf of Mexico. Forecasters at the National Severe Storms Forecast Center couldn't determine exactly where, but they were certain that severe storms would form within twenty-four hours in the middle or lower Mississippi Valley, and they advised local weather station offices throughout the area to be on the alert.

Turn On the Radio!

Some municipalities have contemplated eliminating their tornado siren systems, and many others have eliminated them. If your city no longer has a warning system, then you would be wise to invest in a weather radio that automatically turns itself on when a warning has been issued.

THE PERFECT STORM

Around 2 p.m. Central Daylight Time, two tornadoes touched down at nearly the same moment in Gilmer County, Georgia, and Bradley County, Tennessee. For the next sixteen hours, one tornado after another churned to life, slicing through thirteen states from Mississippi to Michigan. The outbreak was unprecedented in US weather history: in less than twenty-four hours, 148 tornadoes tore across America, six of which grew into giant F5 twisters with winds as high as 318 miles per hour. The previous year, only one F5 storm was recorded in the United States. And some years there are none at all.

Timely Warnings

One of the cities hardest hit by the outbreak was Xenia, Ohio, where an F5 tornado destroyed half the town in just nine minutes. A local television station spotted the approaching twister on its radar scope and broadcast the image of its hook echo, and police cruisers took to the streets with loudspeakers, warning residents to take cover immediately.

The massive tornado entered the city around 4:30 in the afternoon, ripping apart a housing development before leveling the downtown business district, leaving a trail of wreckage 2,000 to 3,000 feet wide. The tornado destroyed schools and businesses with equal fury and went on to demolish 85 percent of Central State University. It took out nine churches and 1,333 homes and businesses, and left thirty-three people dead in the wake of its rampage. After the storm, two hundred trucks a day rumbled through Xenia's rubble-strewn streets to clear away the debris, but the clean-up process still took more than three months. On a wall at City Hall, a small plaque pays tribute to those who died on that terrible day.

Tragedy and Triumph

In all, the super outbreak took 330 lives and injured 5,550 people in a wide swath from Georgia to Illinois, causing damages totaling $600 million in 1974 dollars. By the time it was over, storm warnings had been issued for nearly half a million square miles, and tornadoes had directly affected more than 600 square miles of countryside.

Few would argue that many more lives would have been lost if not for the warnings issued by the National Weather Service and other agencies. Even without the benefit of modern NEXRAD radar and high-resolution satellite images, the Weather Service saved lives by issuing 150 tornado warnings and 28 severe weather watches during the developing disaster, helping to reduce the death toll.

HURRICANE ANDREW

A Swath of Devastation

As a tropical storm, Andrew was something of a bust by the time the first Hurricane Hunter flight reached it on Wednesday, August 19, 1992. Still far out in the Atlantic with no clear center of circulation and rising barometric pressure, Andrew seemed to be a storm looking for a place to die.

But meteorologists at the National Hurricane Center in Coral Gables, Florida, knew better than to turn their backs on the storm. Andrew was moving into an area where strengthening was possible, although none of the computer models agreed on just where it might go. In the early hours of Saturday, August 22, Andrew became the first hurricane of the year. With a large dome of high pressure building to the north of the storm, Andrew had picked up speed and was turning farther to the west by evening, with sustained winds blowing at 110 miles per hour.

HURRICANE ANDREW

Residents along Florida's southeast coast awoke the next morning to find themselves under a hurricane watch, and many went in search of canned food, bread, and other staples, while others stripped home improvement warehouses of plywood. By midmorning the sound of hammers could be heard up and down the coast as windows were boarded up and other last-minute preparations were rushed to completion. Some locked up their homes and drove north or west, away from the approaching storm.

The Threat Intensifies

By noon, Andrew's winds had increased dramatically to a sustained speed of 135 miles per hour, gusting to 165. A crew of meteorologists was dispatched from the National Hurricane Center in Miami to NOAA headquarters in Washington, DC, in case the center was disabled, since it now appeared as if Andrew would score a direct hit there. As night fell, Hurricane Center director Dr. Bob Sheets was the man in demand, fielding questions from a team of television reporters and issuing warnings and reports. On a monitor behind him, viewers watched a radar image of Andrew churning toward Florida like a giant red buzz saw.

As midnight approached, forecasters were alarmed to see that Andrew had gained even more strength as it passed over the warm waters of the Gulf Stream. Now screaming at 145 miles per hour, Andrew's winds were gusting to an incredible 175 miles per hour as it bore down on the Florida peninsula. That same day, Hurricane Center meteorologist Stan Goldenberg's wife had borne their first baby girl, and afterward he had rushed home to help his three sons and his sister-in-law's family prepare for the storm.

Worse to Come

As bad as Andrew was, research scientists say that hurricanes could get a lot worse if the earth's atmosphere continues to heat up. They also speculate that in the event of an asteroid or comet impact, which rapidly heats ocean water, the result could be a "hypercane" 20 miles high with winds near the speed of sound.

In the Teeth of the Gale

Just before 5 a.m., the 2,000-pound radar dome on the Hurricane Center's roof came crashing down after a wind gust of 150 miles per hour. At Goldenberg's home, the winds had ripped plywood shutters from the windows, and flying debris sent glass shards flying into the house. The family fled to the kitchen, but the roof blew off and the walls began to fall around the frightened group. At the Hurricane Center, the howling winds finally destroyed the anemometer after it recorded its final reading: 164 miles per hour.

As dawn arrived the following morning, the winds were finally dying down, and dazed survivors emerged from the wreckage of their homes to a scene many likened to the aftermath of aerial bombing. Most trees were completely gone, and those few that remained were nothing but splintered trunks. The devastation stretched on for miles, with a few homes relatively untouched while others nearby were razed to their foundations. With streets covered with debris and landmarks either gone or unrecognizable, rescue workers became lost as they responded to emergency calls. Goldenberg and his family had survived the night after taking refuge at a neighbor's house, but they returned to their home to find it mostly destroyed, one of its concrete-block walls resting on top of the family car.

ANDREW'S AFTERMATH

The days to follow would be even more trying for residents, as the heat, humidity, and lack of water and electricity took their toll. Dazed homeowners picked through the wreckage, trying to salvage what they could while waiting for government relief workers to arrive. As bureaucrats bickered over what to do and when, Dade County

Emergency Management Office director Kate Hale angrily asked, "Where the hell is the cavalry on this one?"

On Friday, a full four days after Andrew had ripped Dade County apart, 8,000 National Guard troops finally arrived with portable toilets, ready-to-eat meals, tents, food, and other necessities. Earth-moving equipment was brought in to clear streets of debris, and the business of clearing and rebuilding began.

Good versus Evil

The aftermath brought out the best and worst in human behavior. Atlanta-based Home Depot set up three tent stores in addition to its twenty-five Dade County locations and sold the basic products for restoring walls and roofs at cost. Members of the Grocery Manufacturers of America distributed food to hurricane victims free of charge, and cities all over Florida and in other states took up donations for relief supplies. The Charleston, North Carolina, Chamber of Commerce sent a team of disaster-resource specialists battle-hardened by Hurricane Hugo. By the weekend, twelve tent cities were taking shape with room for 36,000 people.

As *The Miami Herald* reporters investigated the damage, they discovered that many newer homes had been lost due to shoddy construction. Dade County building codes are among the most stringent in the country, but the *Herald* found that overworked inspectors were simply unable to cover all new construction adequately. Significantly, it was also discovered that a fourth of campaign contributions during the past decade had come from the building industry.

The Final Toll

Andrew killed fifty-three and caused $25 billion in damage, making it, at that time, the costliest storm in US history. About

125,000 homes were partially or totally destroyed by the storm, and 7,800 businesses were affected, putting 120,000 out of work. The advanced state of hurricane prediction and massive evacuations were the main reasons why the death toll wasn't higher.

There is a common misconception that Andrew was a Category 5 storm, but with its officially recorded 145-mile-per-hour sustained winds, it rated only a 4 on the Saffir-Simpson scale. Nevertheless, Andrew was a wake-up call, not only for south Florida but for all East Coast residents. The last major hurricane to hit the area had been Betsy in 1965, followed by a lull that lasted an entire generation. Andrew brought that period of calm to a violent end, even as it raised the public's awareness of killer storms and made it much less likely that anyone would be caught unprepared by the next one.

HURRICANE FLOYD

High Winds and Flooding

In mid-September 1999, a small tropical disturbance moving west across the Atlantic grew into a 600-mile-wide hurricane that tore through the Bahamas with winds of 155 miles per hour. Florida residents jammed grocery stores and home improvement warehouses as Hurricane Floyd bore down on the peninsula, but the Sunshine State was spared at the last minute as the storm turned north. Not so lucky was the Atlantic seaboard, which bore the full brunt of Floyd as the hurricane surged inland at Cape Fear, North Carolina.

HURRICANE FLOYD

Fortunately, Floyd had weakened in its trip up the coast, and by the time it made landfall, the highest winds were around 110 miles per hour. High winds caused some damage along the coastline, but the worst was yet to come. Hurricane Dennis had lingered off the North Carolina coast only a week before, pounding the eastern part of the state with wind and rain, and the ground was saturated with water. In Rocky Mount, Dennis had dropped 5 inches of rain, and Floyd deposited another 16.18 inches on top of that. In less than a week many areas of the state received more rainfall than they usually saw all year.

Rising Rivers

As the rain continued to fall, already swollen streams and rivers rose even further, overflowing their banks and spreading out into floodplains that had remained dry for more than a hundred years. The flooding spread eastward as the overflowing tributaries carried huge amounts of water downstream toward the sea, virtually wiping out the small town of Princeville, which had been founded by former slaves in 1865. The town was built on the banks of the Tar River, and when the river crested at an estimated 27 feet (estimated because the measuring gauge was completely submerged at that point), Princeville all but disappeared.

Many people had to cut holes in their roofs after being trapped in their attics by rising waters, and Coast Guard helicopters were pressed into service to rescue thousands. Pigs and cattle died in droves, trapped in the flood, and county after county was declared a disaster area. Floyd completely destroyed 7,000 homes in North Carolina alone, and left another 17,000 uninhabitable. H. David Bruton, the state's Secretary of Health and Human Services, said, "Nothing since the Civil War has been as destructive to families here."

Floyd wasn't through with the East Coast yet. Many rivers in southeastern Virginia broke one-hundred-year records as they rose high above flood stage. The rampaging waters left nearly 300,000 people without power, damaged 5,000 homes, and filled downtown Franklin with 12 feet of muddy, smelly water.

Floyd and Hog Farms

One of Floyd's worst effects was felt in eastern North Carolina, which is home to the majority of the state's hog farms. Each day thousands of tons of hog waste and manure are flushed out of hog houses into open-air cesspools. When these lagoons were flooded, millions of gallons of waste poured out of lagoons into rivers and streams, polluting groundwater and posing a serious health threat.

By the time Floyd reached New Jersey, it was a tropical storm with winds of only 60 miles per hour, but its rains had lost none of their punch. The Raritan River Basin in the north-central part of the state received 7–11 inches of rain in less than twenty-four hours, and when the river crested on September 17, it set a new record of 42.13 feet, the highest recorded level since 1800. Tens of thousands of utility customers were without power after the storm, and flooded water treatment plants left thousands more without drinking water. The flooding caused electrical short circuits in many places, and fires began to break out, burning out of control as firefighters tried to reach them by boat.

Floyd took a final swipe at the United States in Maine and New Hampshire, where it dumped another 3–7 inches of rain before exiting into eastern Canada. The storm killed fifty-seven people, mostly deaths by drowning, and caused damages estimated to be more than $6 billion. More than 2.6 million people were evacuated from their homes ahead of the storm—the largest peacetime evacuation in US history—and ten states were declared major disaster areas in its wake.

Organizational Issues

Many of the disaster-relief problems uncovered by Floyd were organizational. The radios in military vehicles called in to help support relief efforts often couldn't communicate with the radios used by civilian disaster workers, for example, and many rescue units were neither equipped nor trained for flood rescue.

Not a Surprise

Hurricane Floyd didn't exactly sneak up on the East Coast. By 1999 satellite and aircraft observation methods were advanced enough to give everyone plenty of warning. Unlike a flash flood, Floyd gave coastal residents several days to make preparations. If that's the case, how could so many people still get caught unaware as floodwaters swept away their homes and families? Weren't any flood warnings issued before the storm?

In fact, the Southeast River Forecast Center (SERFC) in Atlanta was predicting 6–12 inches of rainfall from Floyd the day before it made landfall in the Carolinas, warning that rivers 80 to 100 miles inland would experience record floods. But the media were concentrating on the coastal regions, broadcasting video of thousands of evacuees heading west as the storm advanced. Kent Frantz of the SERFC remembers that "we tried to tell everyone that the main problem was going to be inland flooding, but no one seemed very interested."

KATRINA AND SANDY

Superstorms

In 2005, Hurricane Katrina smashed into the Gulf Coast, resulting in an estimated 1,245 deaths and damage estimated at $108 billion. Seven years later, the East Coast was pummeled by Hurricane Sandy, one of the largest and most destructive storms ever to strike the area. Even with the advances in forecasting and hurricane preparation, these storms showed how destructive weather-related events can still be.

HURRICANE KATRINA

Katrina formed as a tropical depression in late August 2005. It strengthened as it approached land and went from a tropical storm to a Category 3 hurricane. Nine hours later it was classed as a Category 5 storm. At its height, it was sustaining winds of 175 miles per hour. After passing over New Orleans and other parts of Louisiana, it continued into Mississippi as a Category 3, and by the time it reached Tennessee, it had slowed to a tropical depression.

Levees and Lawlessness

On August 28 the mayor of New Orleans, Ray Nagin, ordered the mandatory evacuation of the city, the first in US history. But although many obeyed the order, others remained, determined to ride out the storm. The city relied heavily on a system of levees, most of which had been kept in poor repair. The storm broke through them, and water poured into New Orleans. Eighty percent of the city was flooded. Lake Pontchartrain was badly polluted by waste carried by the floodwaters.

Those who had remained in the city fled to the Superdome sports venue, which became a temporary home for thousands. Conditions within the Superdome rapidly deteriorated, as people suffered from heat exhaustion and the plumbing system broke down under heavy use. Six people inside the Superdome died, although unofficial reports put the number much higher.

Eventually, after several weeks, order began to arise from the chaos. But the federal and state governments were widely blamed for the extent of the disaster. Michael Brown, President Bush's appointee to head the Federal Emergency Management Agency (FEMA), was forced to resign in disgrace, and the events surrounding Katrina badly damaged the Bush administration's standing with the American people.

SUPERSTORM SANDY

Hurricane Sandy ranks second in the history of damaging storms. It struck the East Coast in October 2012 after beginning as a tropical depression in the Caribbean. By the time it reached Cuba, it had strengthened to a Category 3 hurricane. It weakened and then strengthened again, passing along the US coast.

Storm warnings caused widespread evacuations in many states, which helped keep the death toll relatively low (233 people were killed). Nonetheless, the damage caused by the storm was extensive, estimated at $75 billion. Damage was greatest in New Jersey and New York. In New Jersey much of the Jersey Shore was heavily impacted, and thousands of buildings were leveled. In New York City many of the city's subways had to be closed because of flooding when the East River burst its banks.

STAYING SAFE IN THE WEATHER

Planning Ahead

Staying safe from hazardous weather is a lot like playing chess: the further ahead you plan, the more likely you are to win. With lightning, floods, hurricanes, and tornadoes wreaking havoc all over the globe, it sometimes seems the weather is out to get you. But planning for every possible scenario can pay off when disaster strikes.

DODGING THUNDERBOLTS

A powerful thunderstorm is one of nature's most awesome shows, and a vivid lightning display can often send the curious outside to watch. But lightning can travel great distances from its source, and there's really no safe outdoor location when a thunderstorm's around. Research by the National Lightning Safety Institute has shown that there are some places you just don't want to be in or near during an electrical storm:

- In large open spaces or high spots
- In unprotected outdoor structures such as gazebos
- Near any high objects such as telephone poles or flagpoles
- Near any metal objects such as bleachers or fences
- Near bodies of water
- Under trees

Safer places include fully enclosed vehicles such as cars, trucks, and buses, as long as the windows are rolled up and you stay away from any metal parts such as window handles or gearshifts. You may have been told that the tires on your car protect you from lightning because rubber is a good insulator. Air has great insulating properties as well, but lightning blasts right through it. If a bolt of lightning has traveled many miles to reach your car, a couple of inches of rubber aren't even going to slow it down.

Cars As Safety Spots

The reason cars make safer havens in a storm was discovered by Michael Faraday, a nineteenth-century British scientist who found that electromagnetic fields would not penetrate a metal grid. When lightning strikes a metal vehicle, the car protects its occupants by carrying its electrical current through the frame, leaving passengers unharmed.

If you're in a car when a severe thunderstorm strikes, the best thing to do is to pull off to the side of the road, taking care to leave plenty of room between you and the roadway if possible. Then turn off the engine, turn on your emergency blinkers, and wait for the bad weather to pass. If you're in a car with a body made of fiberglass or composite plastics, you should seek shelter in a safer place such as a metal automobile or a building. Although a metal car's frame may protect you, the car itself may not be so lucky: police reports show that lightning can blow out tires, destroy an automobile's electrical system, and, not surprisingly, completely ruin the paint job.

Staying Safe, Inside and Out

The best place to be during a thunderstorm is indoors, preferably in a large building. If the delay between seeing a lightning strike and hearing the thunder is less than thirty seconds, it's time to get away from the windows and find an interior room. Other indoor tips:

- Avoid bathing or using water until the storm passes.
- Stay off the telephone (cordless and cell phones are okay).
- Turn off and unplug appliances, computers, TVs, and power tools.

If you're caught outdoors with no immediate shelter, get to the safest location you can, away from trees, water, and metal. If you feel your hair suddenly standing on end or your skin begins to tingle, there's a good chance a lightning bolt is coming. To make a smaller target, put your feet together and crouch as low as you can. Tuck your head down and cover your ears. When the immediate threat passes, get to a safer place as quickly as possible.

Spread Out

A single lightning strike can kill several people if they're close together. If you're in an outdoor group when lightning threatens and there's no shelter nearby, make sure everyone spreads out so there are several body lengths between each person. If you're at a sporting event or concert, get up and make your way to an exit.

What if, despite your best efforts, someone in your group is hit? Call 911 immediately. The victim may not be breathing, since lightning can cause cardiac and respiratory arrest, so it's vital to maintain brain oxygen levels with cardiopulmonary resuscitation (CPR) and mouth-to-mouth ventilation while waiting for emergency services to arrive. Don't be afraid to touch the victim; no residual electrical charge remains in a person's body after a lightning strike. If you're outside in an active thunderstorm, consider moving the victim to a safer location.

Avoid These Charges

Lightning kills about 10 percent of its victims, and the survivors often suffer long-term effects such as seizures, confusion, weakness, paralysis, and depression. According to data collected by the National Oceanic and Atmospheric Association (NOAA), between 1985 and 2014 an average of 49 people were killed by lightning every year.

A lightning bolt lasts only a fraction of a second, but in that time it can pump 300 kilovolts (300,000 volts) of electricity through a victim. Compare that to the 120 volts carried by your home electrical system, and you can see that there are very good reasons to take cover when the next thunderstorm hits your area.

FLOODS AND TORNADOES

Precautions to Take

The best precaution you can take against living in a flood area is to determine a prospective home's flood history before moving in. But even if you've been in your current location for some time, finding out if you're in a flood-prone area allows you to take precautions you might otherwise forgo. Many residents of eastern North Carolina didn't realize they were living in a one-hundred-year floodplain until after Hurricane Floyd ravaged the region in 1999, washing many homes away and making the area even more unlivable with its muddy floodwaters.

Talk to Someone

To find out if you're in a potential flood zone, contact your local Red Cross chapter, emergency management agency, or National Weather Service office. FEMA also maintains a list of areas that are prone to flooding. The agency's flood hazard mapping helps identify whether a specific location falls in or near a Special Flood Hazard Area (SFHA), subject to inundation by hundred-year floods.

Homeowner's insurance doesn't cover flood damage, so ask your insurance agent how to apply for separate coverage. You could be eligible for insurance via the National Flood Insurance Program, but only if your community has decided to participate. To join, a municipality must agree to adopt and enforce ordinances that restrict construction in floodplains, which helps reduce both flooding damage and insurance rates.

First Steps

Once you know your flooding risk, you're in a much better position to take action when a flood is imminent. If it looks like your area is in for an extended period of rain, filling your car's gas tank is a good first step; when the power goes off, most gas pumps won't operate. Water service may be affected, too, so fill up clean jugs and other containers with water and store them tightly capped. It's good to have at least three gallons of water per person on hand. Buy food that doesn't need refrigeration or cooking, and store it in sealable plastic bins on the higher shelves in your pantry. Most important, make sure you have first aid supplies available.

A good rule of thumb is to keep at least three days' worth of necessities on hand for emergency situations. You can keep all the necessary items in a disaster kit, which should include:

- Extra car keys, cash, and credit cards
- A first aid kit and extra prescription medications
- A cell phone, battery-powered radio, flashlight, and extra batteries
- Two changes of clothing for each person
- Blankets and sleeping bags
- Towels and rubber gloves
- Any special items needed for infants or the elderly

This is where the rest of the family comes in. Before the first storm cloud appears on the horizon, sit down and discuss what each person's responsibility will be in case of an emergency. Pay special attention to family members with special needs, as well as your pets. The more you have settled these issues calmly in advance, the less you'll have to worry about when the time comes.

Write down all the steps to be taken. Select a relative or friend as a contact person, and post that person's phone number, as well as emergency numbers, in a prominent location. If you don't already know, learn how to turn off gas and electric services, and explain the process to the rest of the family. Teach children how to dial 911, and explain when it's okay to call and when it's not.

When It's Not a Drill

When a flood is possible, the National Weather Service will issue a flood or flash flood watch. This means that conditions that can cause flooding are developing in your area, and it's a good time to review your flood plan and be prepared to evacuate if instructed to do so. Move valuables to the higher floors of your home or into an attic if possible.

Get to the High Ground

If you're outdoors when a flood threatens, get to higher ground and stay there until the risk has passed. Get as far away from rivers, storm drains, streams, and creeks as you can. Do not attempt to cross a flowing stream if the water is more than ankle-high.

When a flood or flash flood has actually been reported or is imminent, the Weather Service issues a flood warning. Stay tuned to television or radio broadcasts, and be ready to move at a moment's notice. Have your disaster kit readily available. If told to evacuate, don't delay—get out as fast as you can. Flash floods often leave little time for escape, and evacuation routes can quickly be blocked by rising waters.

Cars Make Lousy Boats

If you're driving, avoid areas that are already flooded or where water is flowing. Below the water's surface, the roadway could be damaged or washed away, and it's often impossible to determine how deep the water is, especially at night.

Nearly half of all deaths caused by flooding happen in automobiles. Because water weighs 62.4 pounds per cubic foot, it exerts tremendous pressure on anything in its way. Every foot that floodwaters rise below a car displaces 1,500 pounds, in effect making the car weigh that much less. Unless a car is already flooded, 2 feet of water can turn a car into a floating death trap, so if your car stalls during a flood, get out immediately.

After a flood, most evacuees understandably want to return to their homes as soon as possible. Although the water may have receded, entering a flooded building may still be hazardous. Electrical wiring may have developed dangerous short circuits and should be inspected and repaired before the power is restored. Floods can also destabilize a building's internal structure, so be cautious until it has been inspected and declared sound. Wearing a hard hat or other protective headgear is always a good idea.

Floods are the number one cause of weather-related deaths in the United States, killing an average of 139 people each year. However, armed with knowledge of your area's flood history and a solid disaster plan, you and your family can avoid the danger when the hard rains come.

TORNADO SURVIVAL 101

If you live on the Great Plains, you're no doubt aware that your area catches the brunt of tornado action each spring. But the Midwest has no exclusive contract with the atmospheric funnel factory; tornadoes can occur just about anywhere, at any time of the day. Tornadoes generally travel from southwest to northeast, but their movement depends on local upper-level winds, and they've been spotted heading in just about all directions.

The giant funnels are not only the most violent storms on Earth but also the most unpredictable, underscoring the need for thorough preparation before tornado warnings flash across your TV screen. The erratic nature of tornadoes means that they can form without warning, so if you see a funnel in the distance, alert the police, a local television station, or a disaster management office immediately; it could help save many lives.

Of course, if you see a tornado forming near you, your own safety should be your main concern. Knowing what to look for is important, because a tornado doesn't always form in a neat Wizard-of-Oz shape, and can even be totally hidden by curtains of rain. Falling hail can be a cautionary sign if your area is under a tornado watch or warning, although hail also falls in severe thunderstorms. Perhaps the most obvious indication is a rumbling or roaring sound that increases in volume; many have said an approaching tornado sounds like a freight train or jet engine.

Spotting a Mesocyclone

If you see ragged clouds rotating around the base of a thunderstorm, it's evidence of a mesocyclone that can give birth to a funnel cloud. Sometimes dust and debris will be kicking up under a storm, even though there's no funnel; that just means the vortex hasn't sucked up enough material to become visible—yet.

As with other types of severe weather, a disaster plan is a must. Know where you'll take cover when a tornado threatens, and practice getting to safety with your family until the process becomes automatic. One of the safest places in your home is a corner in a basement. If you don't have a basement, the next best place is a windowless interior space such as a closet or bathroom on the lowest floor of your home. If there is a siren warning system in your area, make sure your family understands what each type of tone indicates. Show everyone where the first aid kit, fire extinguishers, and emergency numbers are kept. Pick a nearby meeting area for the family to gather in the event the home is destroyed. Select a contact person in another part of town as a check-in point if family members are separated during a storm.

When a tornado watch is issued by the National Weather Service, it means that conditions are ripe for a twister to form in or near the watch area. This is the time to locate your disaster kit and have it handy. Turn on the TV or a radio and stay tuned to a local station for current information.

A tornado warning means that a twister has been spotted on the ground in your area, or is indicated by weather radar. This is when you should activate your family disaster plan. Get away from all windows immediately. Most tornado injuries are caused by flying debris, and glass shards are at the top of the list. There's no need to partially open a window to reduce the air pressure; if a tornado hits your house, it will take care of that for you!

Taking Shelter

When you get to your prearranged safety area, get under something sturdy like a heavy table or workbench, or cover yourself with a mattress, several layers of blankets, or a sleeping bag to protect yourself from flying objects. If you're in the basement, make sure there's nothing heavy such as a piano or refrigerator on the floor directly above you; it could come crashing down if the tornado hits your home.

Mobile home residents should leave as soon as a tornado watch is issued and go to a neighbor's house or other safe place. Although today's manufactured homes are much more well-constructed than they used to be, they're still no safe haven in a tornado. Even if a mobile home is tied down, it is likely to be destroyed by the 200- to 300-miles-per-hour winds a tornado can generate.

Following the Plan

Most schools and businesses have disaster plans and hold drills from time to time, so follow the prearranged plan when a tornado warning comes. You'll no doubt be instructed to get away from windows and take cover in an interior room in the center of the building. Stairwells also make good refuges, since they're built to support heavy weight and provide a means of exit. When you get to a sheltered place, crouch down and protect the back of your head with your arms.

Use Caution

If you must go into a damaged building, don't use a lighter or matches; the twister could have broken gas lines. And watch out for downed electric lines, glass, nails, and other sharp objects; one study showed that 50 percent of injuries from a tornado happen after the fact.

Cars and trucks are not safe refuges in a tornado; if you've ever seen footage of a huge twister tossing vehicles around like toys, you already know that. It's possible you may be able to outrun a tornado in a car if the roads are clear, there's good visibility, and there happens to be an escape route away from the twister. But it's much more likely that rain will block your view and you'll end up in a traffic jam with other fleeing motorists. The best thing to do is pull off the road and seek shelter in a sturdy building. If you're driving in the countryside when a tornado threatens, quickly park the car and run to low ground, away from any object that could fall onto you. Lie facedown and protect your head with your arms.

Take a Pass on the Overpass

You may have seen the dramatic 1991 footage of a television crew taking refuge under a highway overpass as a tornado roared overhead, leaving them unharmed. This has led to a widespread misconception that overpasses are safe hiding places from a tornado. The fact is, the people in the video are extremely lucky to be alive; their tornado was a relatively weak one and it didn't score a direct hit on the overpass where they had taken cover.

Once a tornado has passed, get your family together and wait for emergency crews to arrive; your first aid kit will be useful if there are any minor injuries. If your house has been heavily damaged, it's best to stay out of it because of the danger of collapse.

MAKING A SHELTER

Years ago storm cellars were common in tornado-prone areas, but many newly constructed homes lack them because of the additional cost. Today many homeowners are creating a different type of refuge, either during or after construction of their homes. They're called safe rooms. These strengthened areas within a house have extra fortification to withstand the extreme conditions that come with tornadoes and hurricanes. Additional information about building a safe room is available from FEMA, which has created a guide to building such a shelter. It's available online or by contacting FEMA directly.

Building a Safe Room

A safe room must be anchored to your home's foundation, with strong connections between all of its components to resist being torn apart. It must be readily accessible from all parts of the house, and should be solid enough to withstand the impact of flying wind-driven objects.

If you don't live in a flood-prone area, a good place to put a safe room is in the basement. However, a cellar shelter must have its own reinforced roof, separate from the basement ceiling. Think of a storm shelter as a self-contained shell with a roof and walls that are isolated from your home's structure. That way, if the outside walls of your home are blown away by a hurricane or tornado's winds, they won't take the walls of your safe room with them.

If you have no basement, an interior space such as a closet can be retrofitted as a shelter, as long as you have enough room to add walls and a ceiling that isolate it from the rest of the house. The materials used in shelter construction are readily available from building supply stores, so whether you build a safe room yourself or hire a contractor, finding construction materials shouldn't be a problem. Take extra care selecting a door for your shelter; it's usually the weakest point in a safe room.

HANDLING HURRICANE HAZARDS

Many homeowners would much rather confront a hurricane than a tornado. For one thing, today's advanced forecasting methods and a hurricane's relatively slow forward motion give you some time to prepare, which is more than you can say for flash floods and tornadoes. Still, it's never too early to begin preparations before these tropical behemoths come beating on your door.

Check Your Insurance

If you live in a hurricane zone, the best time to review your disaster plan is before the hurricane season starts in June. Your insurance policy probably covers damage from wind and rain but may carry a special hurricane deductible. Make sure you carry enough coverage to rebuild your home if it's demolished by a storm.

During Hurricane Andrew, many homes' roofs were ripped off and flung through the air like Frisbees. Later it was discovered that some roofs weren't even attached to the frame; builders had relied on gravity to keep them in place. You can inspect your home for this oversight by climbing into the attic and looking for metal straps holding the roof trusses to the walls. Hurricane straps attached firmly to wall studs are a must if you live in a hurricane-prone area.

Bracing trusses with two-by-fours running the length of the roof is also a good idea; each stud should overlap across two trusses.

Long before a hurricane's outer bands begin to sweep across your neighborhood, you should have all your important papers tucked away in a safety deposit box or other secure place, and given copies to a friend or relative who preferably lives in another town or state. Items to stash away include insurance policies, birth certificates, passports, identification cards, irreplaceable photographs and heirlooms, and removable computer media containing backups of your valuable data. Take "before" pictures of your home and any valuable items and store them safely as well.

SHOULD YOU STAY OR SHOULD YOU GO?

It's important to decide exactly where you and your family will ride out the storm well ahead of time. For most people, except those who live in mobile homes and flood-prone areas, riding out the hurricane at home is the preferred course. This is because hurricane shelters will most likely be jammed with refugees if a major storm threatens.

Some find it easier to buy canned goods, snacks, bottled water, and other necessary items before the hurricane season starts, then consume them after the season is over. Doing this can save you a last-minute, desperate journey to the grocery store, only to find long lines and bare shelves. If you intend to cover your windows with plywood shutters, buy them ahead of time, cut them to size, and install the anchors and bolts you'll need to mount them; then store the panels and hardware in an easily accessible location. If you think groceries disappear quickly when a hurricane's coming, just wait until you see how popular plywood can be.

If you must go to a Red Cross shelter, make sure you've exhausted all other options first. Shelters can supply only the most basic of needs, and may not have beds or medical care available. Conditions will probably be uncomfortable at best, and if a hurricane stalls, you could be spending a lot of time in close proximity to hundreds of other people. Unless that sounds appealing, you'd be better off finding a friend or relative to stay with if you can.

THE WIND IS THE ENEMY

Most wind damage caused by hurricanes occurs when wind gets into a structure and blows it apart from the inside, so job #1 is to keep the wind out of your house. The most vulnerable places for wind to enter your home are the doors and windows, so they need special attention before a storm strikes. New impact-resistant laminated windows are available if expense is no object, but shutters are more affordable and work just as well. Precut plywood panels are even less expensive; make sure they're at least three-quarters of an inch thick.

If you own a boat that can't be moved by trailer, secure all deck gear, sails, dinghies, and anything else that could be lost during a storm or damage another vessel. Under no circumstances should you try to ride out a hurricane on a boat, even if it's docked in a marina. After a major storm, it's common to see boats that have sunk, been thrown onto the shore, or been stacked like toys by the wind and storm surge. If your boat is on a trailer in your yard, move it as close to the house as possible, avoiding any trees that might fall when the storm hits. You can do the same thing with your car if you don't have a garage.

If you live in a mobile home, check the straps and anchors that tie it to the ground before you leave for safer shelter. The number of straps required varies by state, but a good rule of thumb is one tie-down at each end and one for every 10 feet of length. Tighten any loose straps to keep the home from shifting during a storm, and make sure the concrete block piers supporting the frame are vertical, not leaning at an angle.

If you live in a multistory apartment building or condominium, be aware that winds are stronger at higher levels. Make sure you know the location of the nearest exit, and if you live in an upper-story apartment, see if you can stay with a neighbor on a lower floor. Many condos are located near the shore and will be evacuated when a hurricane warning is issued. Do yourself a favor and find a safer refuge well before you're forced to leave.

Don't be fooled if the winds suddenly stop and the Sun comes out during a hurricane; that just means you're in the eye of the storm. It might be just a few minutes until the winds return from the opposite direction, possibly even stronger. Even when the storm is finally past, the danger is by no means over. As you venture outside, watch for downed power lines and anything touching them. Snakes, insects, and other animals are often driven to higher ground by a storm, so be careful when clearing debris. When you have time, take "after" pictures of your home and possessions for the insurance adjuster.

You can't control the weather, but by being prepared to act at the first sign of trouble, you and your family can stay one step ahead of whatever the atmosphere has in store.

THE WEATHER AND YOUR HEALTH

The Body As Barometer

As if tornadoes and hurricanes aren't bad enough, the weather can be dangerous in less obvious ways, affecting not only life and limb but also your health and well-being.

ALLERGIES: NOTHING TO SNEEZE AT

Your eyes are red and swollen, your nose is runny, and you've got the mother of all sinus headaches. They seem like classic cold symptoms but could just as easily be an allergic reaction. It's been estimated that up to 20 percent of the population suffers from seasonal allergies, a collection of maladies that doctors call allergic rhinitis. This so-called hay fever usually strikes in spring and can last all the way through summer and into fall, generating an estimated ten million doctor's office visits in the United States each year.

Ragweed: The Culprit

Grasses cause 30 percent of pollen-related health problems from spring through fall, but the primary offenders are weeds, which account for 60 percent of seasonal allergies. Ragweed is one of the worst: a single ragweed plant can produce a billion grains of pollen, each one smaller than the diameter of a human hair.

Allergic rhinitis can be traced to airborne pollen and mold spores, allergens that come from a wide variety of sources. Tree pollen accounts for only about 10 percent of allergies in the United States, striking mainly in late winter through spring. You may have awakened one morning to see a thick layer of yellow or green pollen on your car; it's caused by pine trees and doesn't generally trigger allergy attacks. The real culprits are particles of pollen from deciduous trees such as oak, maple, and elm.

Airborne pollen can travel for hundreds of miles, so pulling up all the suspected plants in your neighborhood may not solve the problem. Ragweed is so tenacious and bent on self-preservation that a dry summer will cause it to stop growing and put all of its energy into the production of pollen. If you suffer from seasonal allergies, close the windows of your home and use an air conditioner, which filters out pollen; dry your laundry in the dryer, not outside on the clothesline; and spend your time outside in the morning when pollen counts are lowest.

RESPIRATORY REBELLION

An even bigger menace is asthma, which affects nearly twelve million Americans and kills around five thousand annually. The most common type is allergic asthma, which is triggered by many of the same environmental factors as allergies. There is also exercise-induced asthma, thought to be caused by dry bronchial tubes, and infectious asthma, which begins after a viral chest infection. The fourth kind is occupational asthma, contracted when workers come in contact with an asthma-inducing substance on the job. Predictably, their symptoms are worse during the week but improve on the weekends.

The condition known as chronic obstructive pulmonary disease (COPD) also causes respiratory problems. The two most common forms of COPD are emphysema and chronic bronchitis. Emphysema is caused by a swelling of the lung's air sacs, or alveoli. Once it occurs, the damage is irreversible. Chronic bronchitis is caused by irritation of the bronchial tubes over a long period of time, thickening their linings and creating shortness of breath and a predisposition to infections. Weather doesn't directly cause COPD—smoking is the usual suspect—but cold air can cause symptoms to worsen.

FORECAST: ACHES AND PAINS

In the 1960s, Dr. Joseph Hollander, emeritus professor of medicine at the University of Pennsylvania, conducted the first controlled study of the weather's effects on people with joint and bone problems. He built a barometric chamber where atmospheric pressure could be controlled, and moved in eight patients with rheumatoid arthritis and four with osteoarthritis. The twelve subjects lived in the climate-controlled chamber for two weeks, and during that time, only one person failed to respond to any weather changes. The seven other subjects found that their symptoms worsened 73 percent of the time when the chamber's humidity was increased and the barometric pressure lowered, establishing a clear link between weather conditions and human discomfort.

Once the link between weather and pain was established, physicians and biometeorologists got to work on finding the causes. Robert N. Jamison, PhD, of Brigham and Women's Hospital and Harvard Medical School in Boston, Massachusetts, explains that there are many possible mechanisms: "Because tendons, muscles, bones, and scar tissue are of various densities, cold and damp may expand or contract them in different ways. Sites of microtrauma may also be sensitive to expansions and contractions due to atmospheric changes. Changes in barometric pressure and temperature may increase stiffness in the joints and trigger subtle movements that heighten a nociceptive [injury-caused] response."

TEMPERATURE AND YOUR BODY

The Cold (and Hot) Truth

When the temperature plummets, your body's systems are stressed as they struggle to maintain a sufficient internal temperature. Your body's first reaction to cold is the constriction of blood vessels in the skin to reduce the amount of heat lost and to divert blood to your vital organs. You may start to shiver, which produces heat through involuntary muscular contractions, and your body releases hormones designed to stimulate heat production. When the length of your exposure to the cold is prolonged, however, your body's core temperature begins to decline and hypothermia results.

Deadly Hypothermia

Untreated, hypothermia can kill. Early signs include numbness in the extremities and a noticeable loss of coordination. The victim will often shake uncontrollably and show signs of mental confusion or apathy. In advanced stages the patient can become incoherent and unable to walk or stand.

When Frost Bites

Frostbite is another very real danger when cold weather hits, and it can also be accompanied by hypothermia. Frostbite has four distinct phases: in the first stage, blood vessels constrict, leaving the affected tissue starved for oxygen. When the tissue temperature drops below 24.8°F, the second stage is marked by the growth of ice crystals in the skin, which damage the tissue's cellular structure. During the third stage, fluid leaks from blood vessels into the damaged tissue, and in stage four the blood vessels clot, cutting off all blood supply and causing massive cell death in the affected area.

Frostbite symptoms are similar to those of hypothermia: the victim feels extremely chilly, with increasing numbness and decreasing coordination. As the damage progresses, fluid-filled blisters form. In cases of severe frostbite, the blisters deepen and become permeated with a purplish fluid. When the tissue is warmed up again, it will often swell and turn darker.

First Aid and Prevention

The best treatment for frostbite or hypothermia is to get the victim to an emergency room or doctor's office as soon as possible. If help is more than two hours away, a frostbite victim's affected body part should be slowly brought back toward normal temperature in water at 100°F to 105°F, and care should be taken not to allow it to refreeze, since permanent tissue damage would almost certainly occur. For cases of mild hypothermia, try to get the victim moving; exercise generates warmth. Build a fire or get the person near a source of heat. For more severe cases wrap the patient in as many layers of dry blankets or wool clothing as possible, and then add a layer of plastic. Try to keep the victim out of direct contact with the ground.

Layer for Safety

To prevent cold-related injuries, wear layered clothing to insulate your body against the elements. Avoid getting wet: water conducts heat away from the body twenty-five times faster than air, especially when evaporation is enhanced by a stiff wind. If exercising or hiking outdoors, stop whatever you're doing and warm the area immediately if you see or feel evidence of a cold injury.

IT'S NOT THE HEAT,
IT'S THE HYPERTHERMIA

The opposite of hypothermia is hyperthermia, when your body can't keep itself cool enough to maintain normal function. An early stage of hyperthermia is called heat exhaustion, when an excessive loss of water causes the body's internal temperature to rise. Someone suffering from heat exhaustion will appear pale and sweaty, and can often be dizzy and experience nausea or vomiting. A victim's skin will sometimes be cold and clammy. The person should be moved to an air-conditioned building, given water or a sports beverage, and be watched for improvement. If no improvements are seen within thirty minutes, an emergency room should be your next destination.

Heatstroke is hyperthermia gone berserk. With heatstroke, the victim's internal thermostat, or heat-regulating system, has broken down. Symptoms include complete disorientation, difficulty walking, cessation of sweating, fainting, and unconsciousness. The victim's skin will be hot and dry, and his pulse rate may rise as high as 160 beats per minute. Because heatstroke can be fatal, a victim should be cooled down as quickly as possible, using ice packs or cool water splashed on the skin. The person's legs should be elevated, and plenty of fluid should be given. If no medical facilities are nearby, the victim should be wrapped in wet clothing or bedding before transport to the nearest hospital.

Cramping Your Style

Less severe than heatstroke or heat exhaustion are heat cramps, but they can still ruin a perfectly good day outdoors. Heat cramps feel like a severe muscle pull in the calves or other muscles, and are usually brought on by exercising in hot weather before you've built up enough conditioning; a lack of fluids can also play a part. The best remedy is rest in a cool place.

Shun the Sun

Sunlight is essential for human survival; it aids in the production of vitamin D, which prevents a disease called rickets, and is a potent mood elevator. But even limited exposure to the Sun's rays can cause sunburn in fair-skinned people and children, and long-term exposure can create wrinkles and leathery skin as well as a very dangerous form of cancer called melanoma.

Your skin contains melanin, a pigment that gives skin its color and provides some protection from UV solar radiation. The more melanin in the skin, the longer it will take to burn: light-skinned people may burn in as little as fifteen minutes in the noonday sun, while darker-skinned people can stay out for hours. But eventually even the most UV-resistant skin will suffer damage from prolonged exposure, and unlike a burn caused by a match or hot stove, a sunburn tends to sneak up on you. The pain may not peak until six to forty-eight hours after exposure, and then your skin can swell, blister, and peel for days.

Doctors recommend wearing a sunscreen with an SPF factor of no less than 15 (about the same protection as a cotton T-shirt) when you spend time outside. Studies indicate that most people apply only half as much sunscreen as researchers do when they're assigning SPF numbers, so be sure to apply the lotion liberally and reapply it after swimming or heavy perspiration.

Umbrellas, hats, and clothing are other good ways to prevent sunburn, and it's a good idea to avoid the beach between 11 a.m. and 1 p.m.—that's the time when the Sun's UV bombardment is at its daily peak. Unfortunately, the effects of solar radiation are cumulative, so the more time you spend in the Sun, the more likely it is you'll eventually have skin problems.

DEPRESSED OR JUST SAD?

There is now little doubt that long periods of gray, gloomy weather can bring on a crushing case of the blahs. This even has a name: seasonal affective disorder, or SAD for short.

SAD Symptoms

Symptoms of SAD include carbohydrate craving, weight gain, oversleeping, and other depressive symptoms such as lethargy and a feeling of hopelessness. The first signs of SAD usually make an appearance in October or November and begin to subside in March or April as spring approaches. Doctors got their first clue into the causes of SAD when some of their patients complained that their depression increased during overcast periods, and they began to look at the effects of different light levels on mood. They found that SAD is more widespread the farther north you go, so people in Seattle are seven times more likely to have it than Miami residents.

Moods and Melatonin

Scientists now think that the release of the hormone melatonin by the brain's pineal gland, a pea-sized structure just below the brain, has a hand in bringing about the change in brain chemistry that causes the symptoms of SAD. Melatonin causes tiredness and seems to be related to our body's biological cycles—called circadian rhythms—although the exact nature of the link is still unclear.

What is known is that SAD patients have more melatonin during a depressive episode than people who are not depressed, and that phototherapy returns their melatonin levels to normal.

Young People Are More Affected

It's now thought that four to six out of every one hundred people may have SAD, and studies show that it's four times more common in women than in men. The malady doesn't usually begin until after a person's twentieth birthday, and the older you get, the less likely you are to contract the disorder.

It's been known for centuries that animals respond to changes in weather: bears hibernate, geese fly south for the winter, and squirrels gather nuts. But for humans, the weather's effect on mood was often chalked up to crankiness or a generally bad attitude. Now the new science of biometeorology is helping explain how climate can have a very real effect on both physiology and psychology, speeding the development of new treatments for weather-related ills.

OUR CHANGING ATMOSPHERE

Humans and Pollution

Humans have been pouring pollutants into the atmosphere ever since the discovery of fire; but volcanoes, forest fires, and even desert dust can add their particles to the mix, creating atmospheric conditions that are hostile to nearly every form of life on the planet. Human effects on the atmosphere translate in the long run into changing weather. This, effectively, is what is meant by the crisis of climate change.

WHAT ARE YOU BREATHING?

Air pollutants fall into two main categories: primary pollutants, which cause a direct effect on the air, and secondary pollutants, which must first mutate into harmful substances such as acid rain and ozone, following a chemical reaction. Primary pollutants come from sources such as smokestacks and auto exhausts, doing their damage immediately on entering the atmosphere.

Approximately 6.6 million tons of pollution are pumped into America's air every year. About 40 percent of it comes from industrial processes, and another 17 percent is emitted by automobile exhaust systems. Particles that can remain suspended in the atmosphere for years are called aerosols. If they're small enough, they can be spread hundreds of miles from their sources by the prevailing winds in the upper atmosphere. The tiniest particles are able to slip right by your lungs' defenses and cause allergic reactions and worse.

In cities the major pollution culprit is carbon monoxide (CO), an odorless, colorless toxic gas that results from incomplete combustion of fuel. Motor vehicles account for about two-thirds of carbon monoxide emissions in urban areas, although the figure can rise as high as 90 percent. Carbon monoxide harms humans and animals by reducing the amount of oxygen blood can carry. Since it can bond more easily with hemoglobin than oxygen, high levels of carbon monoxide in the blood are very difficult for the body's defenses to remove. Low levels of carbon monoxide poisoning create flulike symptoms, while higher levels result in loss of consciousness, convulsions, coma, and finally death.

A Greenhouse Gas

You may not think of carbon dioxide (CO_2) as a pollutant; after all, your lungs produce it with each breath. But it's also a by-product of burning fossil fuels such as oil, natural gas, and coal. Aside from being toxic if inhaled in large amounts, carbon dioxide has been identified as one of the major greenhouse gases.

THE INS AND OUTS OF HAPS AND VOCS

The Environmental Protection Agency (EPA) has identified 188 chemicals that can cause serious effects on human health and the environment, and has assigned them the collective name of hazardous air pollutants, or HAPs. Exposure to these compounds can cause serious disabilities and illnesses such as cancer, diseases of the central nervous system, birth defects, and even death by large-scale releases. The major cancer-causing HAPs are 1,3-butadiene, polycyclic organic matter, benzene, carbon tetrachloride, chromium, and formaldehyde.

The Bhopal Disaster

A major pollution disaster happened in Bhopal, India, in 1984. A release of deadly gases at a Union Carbide pesticide plant there killed at least 1,700 people and injured several hundred thousand others, many who experienced permanent physical disabilities, respiratory ailments, cancers, and multigenerational genetic damage.

Many manufacturing processes, including spray painting, semiconductor manufacturing, dry cleaning, wood finishing, and printing produce volatile organic compounds (VOCs), use a class of chemicals that easily forms vapors at normal temperatures and air pressures. Some of these gases are harmful when inhaled, and many of them are carcinogens. Others are readily soluble in water and can pollute not only the air but groundwater supplies as well.

VOCs are indoor hazards as well: they can be found in paints, solvents, household cleansers, and disinfectants, among other common supplies. Limited exposure can cause headaches and irritation of the eyes, nose, and throat. More prolonged contact can result in nausea; loss of coordination; and liver, kidney, and central nervous system damage.

Sulfur dioxide (SO_2) is a pollutant that can be caused by erupting volcanoes, but it is more commonly created as a by-product of the burning of sulfur-containing fuels such as coal and oil, by the smelting of metal, by paper production, and by other industrial processes. Sulfur dioxide is a colorless gas that is odorless in small concentrations but has a strong smell at higher levels. In water, sulfur dioxide dissolves to form highly toxic sulfuric acid; in the atmosphere, it binds with water molecules and falls as acid rain.

ACID RAIN: A BURNING ISSUE

The term *acid rain* is a misnomer in some cases, because pollutants don't always fall to earth in a wet form. The earth's gravity is constantly trying to pull anything in the atmosphere back to the surface, so acidic gases and particles can make their way to the ground without rain in a process called dry deposition. About half of all acidity in the atmosphere returns to earth in a dry form, so a more accurate term for acid rain is "acid deposition."

Acid deposition can happen hundreds of miles from a pollution source. Particles swept up by the wind can often be transported across state and national borders, making air pollution a global problem, not just a local one. In the United States more than ninety billion pounds of sulfur dioxide and nitrogen oxides are released into the air each year. When this acid binds with water droplets and falls as rain, it carries pollutants into the ground and mixes with particles that have already fallen as dry deposition.

Don't Drink the Water

When acidic water enters streams, lakes, and marshes, it begins to lower their pH levels. Soil and water normally have some capacity to neutralize acid, but in places where the soils have low alkaline levels and precipitation has a high acid content, acidity can quickly overwhelm a watershed's natural buffering capacity. As acid rain flows through soil it liberates aluminum, which is carried into lakes and streams along with polluted water. For fish, low pH and high aluminum levels are a deadly combination.

More than thirty years ago, scientists first became concerned when they noticed that even in remote areas, lakes that were once full of fish had become barren. The US Geological Survey was brought in to determine the reason, and eventually acid rain was pegged as the culprit. The survey established the National Atmospheric Deposition Program/National Trends Network (NADP/NTN), which collects rain and snow samples from across the country and monitors them for acid deposits.

The survey found that rain or snow falling in the eastern United States has a much lower pH level than precipitation elsewhere in the country. In addition, a National Surface Water Survey identified several areas where streams were especially sensitive to acidification, including the mid-Appalachian region, the Adirondack and Catskill Mountains, the upper Midwest, and mountains of the western United States. Acid rain was found to be the cause of acidity in 75 percent of acidic lakes and 50 percent of acidic streams.

Acidic Earth

The effects of acid rain aren't limited to bodies of water; the low pH levels it causes in the soil can slow the growth of entire forests, make leaves turn brown and fall off, and even cause trees to die. In the eastern United States the Shenandoah and Smoky Mountain National Parks have been particularly hard hit. Atop Clingmans Dome in the Smokies a once-proud stand of conifers is now a ghost forest, its denuded trees covered with moss and lichen.

Although acid rain doesn't directly kill trees, it weakens them by damaging their leaves and exposing them to toxic compounds in the soil. Just as it does in fish, acidity stresses trees and plants, making them more susceptible to disease or attack by insects, drought, or cold weather. In high forests such as those in the Smoky Mountains, pollution's effects can be magnified and accelerated by the constant presence of acid fog, which acts to deplete essential nutrients in the leaves of plants and trees.

Oh Say, Can You See?

Acid deposition isn't always noticeable, but it affects everything it touches, even buildings and automobiles. In our nation's capital, monuments made of seemingly eternal materials such as marble are literally being eaten away by acid in the atmosphere. Marble is composed of calcium carbonate, or calcite, which is easily dissolved by even mild acid. Because many of our national monuments are made of marble or limestone, some are slowly crumbling as acid deposition takes its toll. Some of the buildings particularly affected are the Capitol, the Jefferson Memorial, the Lincoln Memorial, and the Federal Triangle buildings.

The Shrinking Visual Range

Reduced visibility has devalued what was once an exciting outdoor experience for an estimated 280 million annual park visitors. In the East, where the visual range used to be 90 miles, it's now only 15 to 25 miles. The visibility in western states has declined from 140 miles to 35 to 90 miles.

Pollution can also cause problems with visibility, creating transportation hazards on the ground as well as increased collision dangers for aircraft. Haze in the atmosphere is created by tiny particles of pollution in the air that can either absorb light or scatter it before it reaches an observer. Once-clear vistas in our national parks are now shrouded in brown or white haze for much of the year.

THE DONORA DISASTER

One of the worst air pollution disasters occurred in 1948 in the town of Donora, Pennsylvania, which lies in the Monongahela River valley. The town's location isn't normally a problem, except on rare occasions when a temperature inversion forms. As warm air rises, it usually carries particles of pollution up into the atmosphere where they're dispersed by wind. But during an inversion, a warm layer of air forms over a cooler, denser layer, trapping pollution near the ground.

That's what happened in Donora in October 1948. The city of 14,000 was a company town, dominated by the US Steel factory where many of its residents worked. Townspeople were used to a certain level of smog, but on that fateful Thursday morning, residents awoke to a thick gray fog that seeped into homes even with the doors and windows closed. One by one, community members began to succumb to the acrid cloud, filling hospital emergency rooms with choking, wheezing victims. Many attempted to evacuate the city by car, but the dense smog and massive traffic jams soon made driving impossible. By Saturday, the town's three funeral homes had no more room for bodies and a temporary morgue was set up. The deadly haze enshrouded Donora for the better part of five days until a rainstorm finally dispersed it.

When the air cleared, twenty people were dead and nearly 6,000 were ill from the smog's effects. Many blamed the steel and zinc works along the river, which had continued to pump fumes into the saturated atmosphere until four days after the emergency began. The disaster led to the first air pollution conference, convened by President Harry Truman in 1950, which raised public awareness of the problem and set the stage for the Air Pollution Control Act, which was passed in 1956. For the first time, the US government identified air pollution as a national problem and announced its intention to improve the situation.

THE CLIMATE CHANGE CONTROVERSY

The Greenhouse Effect

With carbon dioxide and other pollutants being piped into the air all over the world, many scientists believe human activity is causing a slow but inexorable warming of the entire globe. Are humans really to blame, or is the earth just going through another of its natural stages?

A HOT TOPIC

Climate change has become a media obsession, but the earth's climate is variable by nature, and it has gone through drastic changes in its history. In fact just 18,000 years ago (a mere blip in geological time), the North American continent and Europe were in the grip of an ice age, with glaciers extending south as far as New York. So much water was stored in the earth's ice caps that the sea level was up to 400 feet lower than it is now.

Disrupted Energy Balance

The earth's climate reflects the balance of energy between the planet and its atmosphere. You've seen how precipitation, condensation, and wind tend to distribute heat from solar radiation around the globe. Evidence is mounting that the earth goes through regular cycles that disrupt its energy balance and produce extremes of heat and cold.

Of course, at that time the nomadic people who inhabited the land that would become America could migrate south to more temperate climates, but if the glaciers began moving in today, the consequences would be catastrophic. Why does the earth experience such dramatic changes in its climate from time to time? And what—or who—is responsible?

You may have come to think of the greenhouse effect as a bad thing, but were it not for greenhouse gases, the planet's average temperature would be about 61°F colder than it is now. It's important that a certain amount of heat be trapped near the surface, or summer would turn to winter, and winter would be—well, you get the idea.

IS THE EARTH RUNNING A FEVER?

During the twentieth century, the earth's average temperature increased by about 1°F, with half of that rise taking place between 1975 and 2000. The last few decades have seen the warmest summers in the Northern Hemisphere since about A.D. 1000 or perhaps even earlier. In addition, the sea level is rising at the rate of up to a foot per century.

All these symptoms indicate a warming trend, just as a high thermometer reading indicates that a patient has a fever. But the fact that someone has a high temperature doesn't tell the doctor what's causing it, and the same is true of global warming. There's little doubt the earth is getting warmer, but the debates over the cause are hotter still.

Spin Cycles

A Serbian astronomer named Milutin Milankovitch proposed one theory back in the 1930s that involves three components of the earth's position in space. The planet's orbit isn't a perfect circle, but more of an oval, or ellipse. Over a period of 100,000 years, the orbit becomes more and then less elongated, changing the distance the Sun's energy must travel to reach Earth. This process, called eccentricity, reduces and then increases the effect of solar radiation on the surface over time.

Precession, the slow wobble the earth makes as it spins on its axis, is the second part of the theory. Over a period of about 26,000 years, the north polar axis describes a narrow circle in the sky, first pointing to Polaris (the North Star), and then Vega. This changes the seasons in which the earth is closest to the Sun, and the theory predicts that a significant seasonal and climatic alteration results.

The third component of Milankovitch's theory is the earth's tilt on its axis, known as obliquity. This degree of tilt changes as well, from 21.5 to 24.5 degrees over a period of 41,000 years. The planet is now in the middle of the cycle, but as the tilt increases or decreases, the difference in warmth between polar and equatorial regions changes, affecting the severity of the seasons.

The Evidence Mounts

The three components are collectively known as Milankovitch cycles. The scientist theorized that when parts of the three variables occur at the same time, their combined effects are responsible for major climate changes. In the 1970s, NOAA's CLIMAP (Climate: Long-Range Investigation, Mapping, and Prediction) project, which aimed to develop a detailed climatological map of the ancient world using computer modeling, found evidence in deep-sea core samples that substantiated Milankovitch's theory. The samples showed a strong correlation between long-term climate variations and Milankovitch cycles.

Further studies have shown that ice ages reach their peaks every 100,000 years or so—the same amount of time it takes for the earth's orbit to stretch and contract. Examination of ice sheets in Earth's colder regions also indicates that there was about 30 percent less carbon dioxide in the air during ice ages, adding a cooling effect to the atmosphere that could have reinforced and lengthened the colder period.

Will Ice Ages Happen Again?

Because recurring ice ages are one of Earth's regular cycles, it's not only possible there'll be another one, it's inevitable. They only happen once every several thousand years, though, so don't break out the parkas just yet.

POSITIVE FEEDBACK
AND SHIFTING PLATES

Once the earth enters a warming phase, certain atmospheric effects can help sustain the change. If the surface temperature is slowly rising, more and more water will evaporate from the oceans, saturating the atmosphere with tons of extra vapor. With more water vapor in the air, the absorption of infrared radiation speeds up, heating the atmosphere and increasing the rate of evaporation even more. Self-sustaining processes like this are known as positive feedback mechanisms.

One way that climate changes can take place is through the redistribution of the earth's landmasses. According to the theory of plate tectonics, the planet's continents ride on a layer of molten magma, and although the annual rate of motion is only a few inches, over millions of years continental plates can move considerable distances.

Before the continents broke apart and began drifting, the theory states, they were grouped together in a huge landmass called Pangaea. Some scientists think this large area gathered so much snow in colder periods that it reduced average temperatures over the entire globe. Another factor could be continental uplift, the process that formed the Tibetan Plateau. Newly raised mountains and plateaus could have disrupted prevailing winds and caused other drastic changes in the atmosphere. And as continents broke apart, ocean currents would have shifted, creating deserts in some places and rain forests in others.

Continental Drift

Continental drift causes monumental stresses to build up underground, resulting in earthquakes. Many observers have reported strange "earthquake lights" during these events. Although there is no definitive cause for these events, some researchers think that seismic stresses may generate high voltages that are then released into the atmosphere.

Another way that creeping continents can disrupt the atmosphere is through volcanic degassing, which happens when one continental plate meets another. This often takes place deep in the ocean at boundaries called ridges, where molten material from deep in Earth's mantle rises to the surface, spreading out as the plates retreat from each other. If the plates collide, the heavier one will be pushed downward, where it begins to melt. Either way, large quantities of carbon dioxide are produced, enhancing the atmosphere's heat-retaining ability over the long term.

HUMANS GET INTO THE ACT

Nature has been dumping CO_2 and other gases into the atmosphere for eons, but until the beginning of the Industrial Revolution, humanity's primary contribution was ash and smoke from wood fires and methane emissions from farm animals. In the 1700s that began to change with the invention of the coal-fired steam engine, steamboats, and locomotives. Suddenly, transportation was faster and more economical, and with the advent of coal-fueled factories, goods could be produced much more efficiently, at lower cost, and in greater quantities.

The downside, of course, was pollution. But there was a seemingly limitless supply of air, and with mankind now the master of nature (or so it was believed), few gave atmospheric contamination a second thought. As a result, much damage was done before the problem was identified.

Rising Seas

A rise in the sea level increases the likelihood and severity of coastal flooding, and has harmful effects on marshes and wetlands along the shore. It can destroy animal habitats and cause saltwater intrusion into aquifers, thus polluting water supplies. The economic effects can be truly disastrous, making beaches and businesses in tourist areas literally disappear.

Within the past several decades the subject of global warming and climate change has become a priority in many countries. In 1988 the United Nations and the WMO formed the Intergovernmental Panel on Climate Change (IPCC) to monitor the earth's atmosphere and study the effects of humanity's influence. The IPCC is made up of scientists from all over the world; their job is to assess the possible impacts of climate change and inform national leaders of their findings.

In 2013 the IPCC released a report that affirmed its previous position: global warming is real and is changing the earth's climate in ways that natural processes cannot. According to the agency, mankind is now in the midst of a long-term environmental experiment that could have serious negative consequences in the years ahead.

APOCALYPSE: SOON?

Proponents of the global warming theory predict that as the earth continues to heat up and more greenhouse gases are released into the atmosphere, the rate of temperature increase will accelerate. They predict a rise in the average global surface temperature on the order of 1°F to 4.5°F over the next fifty years, as compared with the 1°F increase during the entire twentieth century. During that time, the sea level rose 4–8 inches, and the EPA estimates it could rise another 12–18 inches by 2100. The IPCC's prediction range is 3.5–34.6 inches. Some scientists even think that with enough sustained warming the West Antarctic Ice Sheet could slide into the sea, raising ocean levels up to 20 feet.

A Global Hothouse

As temperatures increase, more frequent and intense heat waves could cause heat-related deaths to soar. The heat would also aggravate pollution problems, causing more respiratory distress and other illnesses. Forests and farmland could be swallowed up by expanding deserts, reducing crop output and causing an even greater temperature spike.

The loss of plant life would reduce the earth's ability to remove carbon dioxide from the air, amplifying the greenhouse effect. Higher temperatures and rainfall amounts would also increase deaths from insect-borne diseases such as malaria and the West Nile virus, which first appeared in the United States in 1999. And with vegetation drying up in the hotter regions, wildfires could run amok across the globe.

The amount of heavy precipitation over land has also increased during the past century, a trend that some scientists say will speed up as the earth warms. Their theory: increased warmth will result in more evaporation, directly generating more rain and snow, causing increased flooding in some areas. With higher sea surface temperatures would come more frequent and much stronger hurricanes, since much more warm water vapor would be available to feed the giant storms.

THE CAUSES OF GLOBAL WARMING

What's to Blame?

The global climate has been in flux throughout recorded history. Could the changes we see happening today be a result of natural processes that have occurred over millennia? Not a chance, say most scientists.

For one thing, they point out, carbon dioxide created from natural sources such as volcanoes still retains a measure of the radioactive element carbon-14, while carbon dioxide released from the burning of fossil fuels does not. In addition, studies performed between the 1950s and the present indicate that levels of this nonradioactive carbon dioxide have risen each year. This evidence, say scientists, can be seen in the decreasing amount of radioactive carbon dioxide captured in tree rings during that time.

Bubbles in ice trapped below the earth's ice caps have produced samples of prehistoric air in core samples brought to the surface, and researchers say they show that atmospheric carbon dioxide was 25 percent less plentiful 10,000 years ago than it is today. The key: that level remained constant over thousands of years instead of showing the steady rise we see today. Some scientists are certain that the actions of human beings are the cause for this increase.

THE OPPOSITION WEIGHS IN

Balderdash, say critics: most of these CO_2 emissions would still take place even if there were no humans on Earth at all, and blaming people for global warming is too simplistic a solution for such a complex problem. They argue that the intricate relationships among all the atmosphere's elements make the creation of a truly accurate climate change model impossible. They point to a competing study that examined ice core samples and concluded that CO_2 levels *did* fluctuate during the preceding 10,000 years. Besides, they say, CO_2 accounts for only 10 percent of the greenhouse gases in the atmosphere; the major culprit is water vapor.

Benefits of Global Warming

Some scientists theorize that global warming could actually be beneficial, bringing relief to snow-prone areas in the winter and reducing the number of annual deaths due to hypothermia. Warmer weather would also bring longer growing seasons, increasing crop yields, and more carbon dioxide in the atmosphere would make plants more vigorous.

Are you confused yet? So is everyone else, but with 6.6 tons of greenhouse gases being emitted for each man, woman, and child in the United States each year, some say the "better safe than sorry" approach of reduction is the best policy. America is the earth's second-largest source of CO_2 pollution, and the rate is increasing—one reason why Congress established the US Global Change Research Program in 1990.

Creating more bureaucracies is certainly one way to attack the issue, but other ways of reducing carbon dioxide emissions have been proposed. One is carbon sequestration, which the US Department of Energy thinks could be used to cut carbon dioxide emissions by a billion tons a year by 2025 and 4 billion tons by 2050. The method proposes to get rid of carbon dioxide by dumping it into the ocean, which is already the earth's major carbon dioxide holding area. The seas contain more than 45 trillion tons of carbon, but scientists say there's room for a lot more.

The process involves pressurizing and chilling carbon dioxide, then pumping it deep into the sea. Sinking to the bottom, it spreads out and thins, eventually dissolving into the seawater. Tests indicate the carbon dioxide dissolves slowly enough to leave sea life unharmed, but fast enough that it doesn't form thick pools that could smother bottom-dwelling plants and fish. Other scientists say it would be easier and just as effective to pump carbon dioxide back into the ground where it came from, and tests are under way to examine that possibility.

CLIMATE CHANGE FROM SPACE?

Many scientists say that to better understand why the earth is warming, you have to look at its main source of heat: the Sun. As with any other global warming theory, the effect of the Sun's influence is still being debated, but many researchers feel that solar variability could be responsible for at least a third of the temperature rise seen in the past century.

But isn't the Sun's energy output a constant? Not really. To astronomers, our Sun is known as a variable star, because its production of radiation varies in a cycle that lasts an average of eleven years, a pattern discovered by amateur astronomer Heinrich Schwabe in 1843. That variation is small—only about 0.1 percent—but it's thought that the fluctuation has been greater over longer time scales, changing by as much as 0.5 percent.

The Sun: A Changing Face

Recently, scientists have discovered statistical links to the Sun's energy output and the number of sunspots on its face. Examining historical records, they found that in the period between 1640 and 1720, the number of sunspots fell dramatically, and so did the earth's average temperature, plunging an average of 2°F. The effect was particularly noticeable in Northern Europe, where glaciers advanced southward and winters were especially harsh.

Sunspots are relatively cooler areas in the Sun's photosphere, so it would seem that fewer sunspots would mean a hotter Sun and hence a warmer atmosphere here on Earth. Once solar-observing satellites were able to examine sunspots closely, however, the mystery was solved: the bright areas called faculae, which accompany sunspots during the solar cycle, are much hotter than sunspots and more than make up for their cooling effect.

Another possible solar effect on climate could be the fluctuation in the UV part of the spectrum, which is much more wildly variable than visible light. During a peak in the Sun's eleven-year cycle, UV radiation increases by a few percent, compared with the 0.1 percent increase in total radiation. Most of it is blocked by the upper atmosphere, but because all the atmospheric layers are connected, constant UV bombardment can affect the amount of ozone in the stratosphere. That effect eventually propagates down to the surface, so UV radiation could be another component of the climate change riddle.

Twisting in the Solar Wind

The Sun also ejects vast amounts of charged particles and magnetic radiation, also thought to have an effect on Earth's climate. This flood of energy—the solar wind—constantly streams past Earth, flowing around the planet's magnetic field. During periods of solar maximum output, the Sun's magnetic field is stretched past the earth, helping to block cosmic rays from entering the atmosphere. But during quieter phases, more cosmic rays leak through.

Some scientists suggest that an increase in cosmic rays can affect the amount of clouds and rain, having a direct effect on the earth's temperature. It was recently discovered that high levels of cosmic ray activity cause the upper atmosphere to become highly conductive, leading to higher electrical charges in water droplets, causing more rain. The proof, they say, is found in the increased carbon-14 levels caused by cosmic rays that have been recorded in tree rings.

In addition to passing through its cycles, the Sun is also moving through space at around 486,000 miles per hour, dragging the solar system with it. At that speed, it takes the Sun about 226 million years to complete one revolution around the Milky Way Galaxy. The last time the Sun was at the present spot in its galactic orbit, humans didn't exist yet, and dinosaurs were the dominant species on the planet.

THE COSMIC MERRY-GO-ROUND

Interesting, but what's our galactic orbit got to do with global climate change? Well, as the solar system orbits in the galactic plane, the flat disk in which the galaxy's spiral arms are found, it bobs up and down like a cork. So every thirty million years or so, the entire solar system passes through a thicker layer of interstellar dust, gas, and debris. During the passage, it becomes much more likely that the Sun will encounter large bodies like other stars and planets, and when this happens their gravitational effects can have a powerful influence on the solar system.

As a large body passes near the Oort cloud, which is a gigantic halo of rock and ice fragments that orbits out past Pluto, some of these objects are slowed or sped up by gravitational attraction, either ejecting them from the solar system or causing them to fall inward toward the Sun. As these celestial missiles enter the inner solar system, they pose an increased danger of collision with Earth. Another effect a passage through the Milky Way's spiral arms might cause is higher-than-normal concentrations of dust falling into the Sun, causing it to burn brighter and hotter, which would increase the amount of solar radiation received by the earth and so increase the average temperature of the atmosphere.

Death Rays

In 1967 another potential source of climate disturbance was discovered when scientists were studying data from satellites looking for Nuclear Test Ban Treaty violations. Instead of radiation from Earth, they found several sources of intense gamma ray bursts coming from outer space. Gamma rays are the most intense form of energy known. Since then, researchers have been unsure of what causes the bursts—called GRBs for short—but increasing evidence indicates they may be the result of supernovas, which are the explosive deaths of massive stars.

When a giant star collapses, it causes an explosion so violent that for a few moments it becomes the brightest object in the universe. The blast creates an intergalactic shock wave that expands outward in all directions like a giant bubble while the star's interior collapses on itself, often forming a black hole. A new theory states that another, faster jet of material from the dying star moving at nearly the speed of light can overtake that bubble's outer boundary, causing a second explosion, which generates a GRB.

An Uncommon Threat

Although astronomers have located GRBs only in other galaxies, it is thought they were once more common in the Milky Way and could have affected ancient Earth's climate. Be glad they're not common today: GRBs can release more energy in ten seconds than the Sun will generate in its entire ten-billion-year lifetime! Scientists think a GRB in our galaxy could have serious consequences for life on Earth.

Put in that perspective, slow global warming doesn't sound quite so bad. Certainly, much more research is needed to determine whether the changes seen in Earth's climate during the past few decades are a result of natural processes or if mankind's recent industrialization is lending a hand. Until then, expect the debate to continue unabated.

TODAY'S TECHNOLOGY

Weather Forecasting's Future

"Forecast for tonight: dark. Continued dark through tonight with scattered light in the morning."

—George Carlin as Al Sleet, the Hippy-Dippy Weatherman

Interpreting the vast amounts of data being gathered by the National Weather Service and other agencies is a huge job. Most radio and television stations have come to depend on specialized weather products, created by private-sector companies, to help them boost ratings by providing dazzling high-tech graphic displays.

BROADCASTING SHENANIGANS

The very first US weathercast took place in New York City on October 14, 1941, as World War II raged overseas. Consisting of a few lines of text, it was transmitted by experimental television station WNBT-TV, which later became WNBC. The forecast was announced by a cartoon character named Wooly Lamb, and was sponsored by Botany Wrinkle-Proof Ties, establishing a lighthearted approach to TV weathercasting that continues today.

After the war the weather forecast became a staple of broadcast news. As the new medium gained viewers, competition increased and stations began to hire professional meteorologists and other on-air personalities to handle their forecasting duties. Many of them were discharged veteran Weather Bureau officers, but many more were hired for their personalities or attractiveness, and some were just clowns, dressing in silly costumes on the air. Although they amused war-weary audiences, appalled meteorologists felt their credibility was on the line.

That's why the American Meteorological Society (AMS) established its seal of approval in 1957. To earn one, a candidate had to pass a series of rigorous tests and be able to not only adequately explain the processes that create various weather conditions, but also to produce a forecast based on those patterns. The applicants' test results were reviewed by a board of AMS members, performance was graded, and the candidates who received a seal of approval could move from station to station without reapplying.

Approved Weathercasters

Since the seal was established, the AMS has certified nearly a thousand weathercasters. A seal of approval is also issued by the National Weather Association, which, unlike the AMS, offers skilled weatherpeople without degrees an equal opportunity for certification.

With no digital 3-D maps or satellite loops yet in sight, early weather broadcasters came up with some ingenious ways of reporting the forecast graphically. In the book *Air Apparent: How Meteorologists Learned to Map, Predict, and Dramatize Weather*, author Mark Monmonier quotes TV meteorologist Gary England as he recalled his first broadcast for an Oklahoma station that used large rotating drums for its maps:

"The metal weather maps on the large four-sided drums somehow looked larger that night. Each drum weighed 180 pounds but felt much heavier. Every time I turned a drum, some of the letters and numbers would fall off or would assume a crazy tilt and have to be rearranged. It was frustrating those days, the norm."

Some weathercasters drew a series of weather maps on large paper charts and flipped through them one by one during their broadcasts, while others developed sliding panels to display their charts. Meteorologist Don Noe of Miami's WPLG created animated maps using stop-motion photography long before it was done with digital technology.

TECHNOLOGY TAKES OVER

In the 1950s, inventor Petro Vlahos developed a system of matting—inserting one picture into parts of another—that was eventually used in movies such as *Mary Poppins*. Vlahos's invention, called chroma key, allowed a television station to insert their on-air meteorologist into a weather map or other background in a process called compositing. It soon became a standard part of most weather broadcasts during the 1970s and 1980s. Vlahos continued to refine the process, and today his company Ultimatte provides digital compositing products for both television and motion pictures.

Today, visuals are king in the world of television weathercasting. Technically advanced graphics quickly and easily explain complex climatic events to viewers, while radar loops and animated satellite images give them immediate feedback on what's going on in the atmosphere.

3-D Weather Mapping

In the late 1980s and early 1990s, advances in computer technology allowed companies such as Earthwatch Communications to develop detailed, high-resolution 3-D weather maps and other high-tech products. Some stations that were still producing their own graphics were dismayed to see their competitors adopting these third-party offerings, as viewers came to expect dazzling eye candy with their daily dose of weather news.

THE LOCAL CONNECTION

The Weather Company is a firm that specializes in forecasting. A subsidiary of IBM, it owns and operates Weather.com, Intellicast .com, and Weather Underground. They are extensively used by companies that need weather-related data to make everyday business decisions. In their words, "We aggregate the deepest, richest data sets—both business and consumer—to deliver personal, reliable and actionable weather information, analytics and insight."

The Weather Company is only one of a number of sources of forecasting and weather-related information that have sprung up. Many smartphone apps have been created to help with predicting and tracking weather. Among them are:

- **Weather Underground.** Owned by The Weather Company, this app taps into a worldwide network of more than 200 weather stations. These measure a wide variety of data and correlate it for you to see. You can get hourly forecasts and forecasts that extend out to about a week's worth of predictions. A separate app, Storm, also from Weather Underground, forecasts the track of an oncoming storm over five hours.

- **Dark Sky.** This app draws its data from NOAA. Based on this, it forecasts local weather. There's not a lot of longer-term forecasting; the focus is on here and now—what the weather's going to do in the next hour or so. You can pull back from the purely local weather to see what's happening on a city, state, country, and global level.

- **RainAware.** As the name implies, the focus is on precipitation in your area. This data comes from a variety of different sources to show you the likelihood of showers, rainstorms, snow, etc. in your immediate vicinity. It can forecast for twenty-four hours or out to seven days. One feature shows you not only what the weather around you is doing, but also the nearest rain to you that's falling.

- **RadarCast Elite.** This app gives a very limited forecast, showing what's going on now, what happened in the past two hours, and what's going to happen in the next hour. There are various layers that can be added to the high-definition radar, which is generated using data from a variety of sources. These layers will show things such as storm intensity, direction, and possible paths. The app also shows where lightning is striking near you.

- **NOAA Radar Pro.** This app will not only give you real-time images on an interactive radar map; it will ding you when a significant weather event is headed in your direction. The app is compatible with the Apple Watch, in case you like your wrist pinging you about the weather.

- **Yahoo Weather.** This free app offers interactive radar as well as a five-day forecast and various satellite maps. The app prides itself on being user-friendly.

Intellicast

Online, The Weather Company offers Intellicast.com (www.intellicast.com), a site that provides twenty-four-hour weather coverage and a multitude of graphic, color-coded maps, charts, and satellite images.

For those who might be considering broadcast meteorology as a career, one experienced meteorologist has this advice: get the best education you can. "Don't be afraid of the math and science," she says. "People don't wake up knowing how to do calculus—they have to learn it." Once the educational requirements are taken care of, the key to getting a job is persistence, she says: "It's a very competitive field, and you really have to be able to sell yourself to the person who's doing the hiring."

Working for the Government

Although television probably comes to mind when you think of meteorologists, the US government is by far the largest employer of weather professionals in this country. NOAA, NASA, and the Department of Defense are just some of the agencies that employ meteorologists.

CONQUERING CABLE

Now a household name, The Weather Channel (TWC) was the brain-child of John Coleman, the first weathercaster for ABC's *Good Morning America* program. In the late 1970s, Coleman became frustrated with the short time he was allotted for each broadcast—usually only two or three minutes—to convey weather information for the entire United States.

Encouraged by a public survey showing that there was a great interest in weather among viewers, Coleman noted that cable television was making rapid inroads in the broadcast industry. Coleman began approaching potential backers, using products like SuperRadar to prove that the technology was in place to provide twenty-four-hour weather information for cable TV.

Virginia-based Landmark Communications, a privately held media firm that owned several newspapers, television stations, and other information outlets, agreed with Coleman, and on May 2, 1982, The Weather Channel was launched. It wasn't exactly an auspicious debut: only four advertisers were on board to pay the fledgling channel's expenses, and the company narrowly avoided disaster in its first year, when it reported a loss of $10 million.

Turning the Corner

In 1983, the company revamped its offerings and began to be picked up by more cable operations. It finally turned a profit in the late 1980s, and has since become the country's leading source of broadcast weather information.

With the availability of twenty-four-hour weather TV came the emergence of a new kind of viewer: the weather addict. According to The Weather Channel, people with a deeper interest in climate and weather comprise 41 percent of the American public, and that curiosity isn't easily satisfied. A Weather Channel press release put it this way:

"Seemingly, the more TWC viewers learn, the more they want to know; some of these people look to the all-weather network with the same interest and enthusiasm some television viewers devote to watching movies. According to Jim Alexander, former vice president of research for TWC, 'A segment of the TWC audience is particularly interested in understanding the mechanisms that influence weather patterns and the meteorological background behind a tornado or hurricane.'"

Web Weather

Weather fans were granted even faster access to their favorite subject when The Weather Channel launched its website, www .weather.com, in April 1995. Currently, the site allows visitors a host of weather-related features including short- and long-term weather forecasts, a variety of weather maps, and specialized forecasts for activities like skiing, fishing, home and garden, and sports and recreation. The Weather Channel app for mobile devices provides forecasts, interactive radar, and real-time alerts.

The Weather Channel now has a radio network that reaches 84 percent of US radio markets, and a service that provides customized weather packages to newspapers across the United States. The channel's web presence has expanded to include the United Kingdom, Brazil, Portugal, Spain, and the US Latino market. The Weather Channel also broadcasts severe weather alerts to mobile device users. For a company once on the verge of bankruptcy, it's come a long way.

INDEX